A GUIDE T
GLASTONBURY'S
TEMPLE of the STARS

Their Giant Effigies Described
from Air Views, Maps, and from
"The High History of the Holy Grail"

by K. E. MALTWOOD

REVISED EDITION
1950
Illustrated by Fifteen Maps

List of Illustrations

1. The Circle of Giant Effigies.

2. Plan on back of former, showing the position of the star constellations.

3. The head of the Lion.

4. The head and breast of the Virgin, and Wheat sheaf.

5. The tail of the Scorpion, and right Claw.

6. The back of Hercules astride the neck of his horse, forming Sagittarius.

7. Map of the Sea Moors of Somerset—"The Kingdom of Logres."

8. The Phœnix Water-bearer.

9. The Fishes and Whale.

10. Three points in the Centre of the great effigy Circle.

11. The Dove.

12. The Ram or Lamb with traditionally reverted head and foot.

13. The Bull's head and right hoof.

14. The Little Dog, and the great Hound.

15. The Griffon, and Poop of Ship.

16. The Giant Orion.

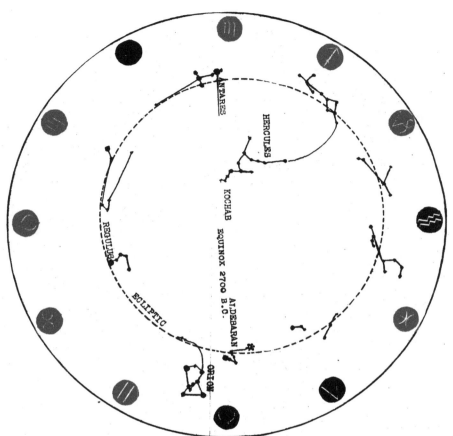

Showing the position of the Stars in the Constellations that correspond with their correct effigies on Plate 1.

[See front which corresponds]

Plate 2

EAST

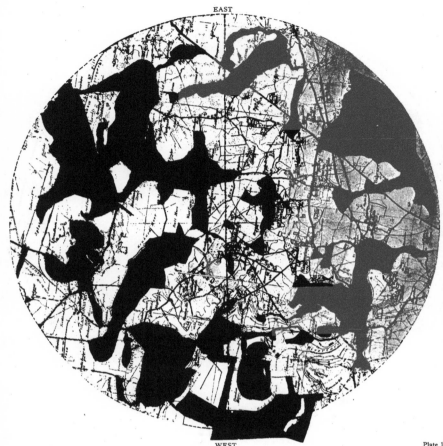

WEST   Plate 1
The Zodiacal Giants of Somerset correspond with the Stars of their respective Celestial Constellations.   [*See back*]

Contents

	Introduction	1
1.	The Fire Sign, Leo	15
2.	The Earth Sign, Virgo	29
3.	The Water Sign, Scorpio	39
4.	The Fire Sign, Sagittarius	43
5.	The Earth Sign, Capricornus	56
6.	The Air Sign, Aquarius	63
7.	The Water Sign, Pisces	76
8.	The Fire Sign, Aries	97
9.	The Earth Sign, Taurus	105
10.	The Dogs	112
11.	Argo Navis, and the "Griffon"	118
12.	Orion the Giant	128
	Bibliography	136
	Subject Index	138

Acknowledgment

Concerning a subject so ancient and so vast, it is only possible to make a few suggestions now for others to verify later, but indebtedness to all sources that have been drawn upon in the compilation of these notes, is here most gratefully acknowledged. Especial thanks are due to those keen aviators whose air views show these ancient landmarks of a forgotten civilization, and thus amplified what the Ordnance Survey Maps had for long delineated, unknowingly.

Corrections, and further information would be very welcome regarding the original names of fields within the specified area; its folklore; items of archaeological and astronomical interest in this connection; as well as Templar and Masonic traditions that bear upon the subject, for:

" . . . now the Holy Thing is here again
Among us, brother, . . .
That so perchance the vision may be seen
By thee and those, and all the world be heal'd."
                                        Tennyson's *Holy Grail*.

I have pleasure in thanking Messrs. J. M. Dent and Sons, Ltd., for permission to quote extensively from **The High History of the Holy Graal** translated by Sebastian Evans; and I should like to acknowledge my indebtedness to many other works, which have helped me, full details of which appear in the Bibliography.

                              K. E. MALTWOOD.

BY THE SAME AUTHOR
Air View Supplement to this Guide
The Enchantments of Britain
King Arthur's Round Table of the Zodiac
Itinerary of 'The Somerset Giants'

Introduction

THE ROUND TABLE was constructed, not without great significance, upon the advice of Merlin. By its name the Round Table is meant to signify the round world and round canopy of the planets and the elements in the firmament, where are to be seen the stars and many other things."—**La Queste del Saint Graal.**

Time and opportunity are given to few to quest Merlin's Round Table of the Grail in the Valleys of Avalon; if then the summing up of many years of adventure in that pursuit is placed at the beginning instead of the end of this Guide, it is in order that those who are neither interested in exploring the heart of Somerset nor in acquainting themselves with its ancient gods, may be spared the topographical details; for it is now possible to localise the Arthurian Grail legends by means of photographs taken from the air in conjunction with the 6 inches to 1 mile Ordnance Survey maps of the district between Somerton and Glastonbury, because in this neighbourhood of the Lake Villages there are prehistoric earthworks and artificial water courses which have at last given up Merlin's secret.

Looking down upon them from the air, with the aid of these maps, it can be seen that they delineate enormous effigies resembling Zodiacal creatures arranged in a circle (Plate 1), as we shall find, they differ very little from the constellation figures and the corresponding stars fall within their boundaries (Plate 2). It is around these archaic Nature Giants that the Arthurian romance accumulated.

For the term effigy in this respect, it is simplest to turn up "Mound Builders" in the **Encyclopædia Britannica,** which says: "In Wisconsin the most interesting mounds are the effigy mounds—earthen forms of mammals, birds, and reptiles, usually in groups and of gigantic size." The **National Geographic Magazine** for May, 1932, reproduced a fine air view of Ohio's "Great Serpent," which measures more than 1,300 ft. from head to tail; there is one somewhat similar in Argyllshire, Scotland. But King Arthur's Woodland Monsters are much larger.

The ancients were familiar with like earthen forms, they spoke of Dragons "of such extent that grass grew upon their backs;" some they said were "five acres" large, and others so great "that riders on opposite sides could not see each other." Though they are found in many parts of

1

the world, it is doubtful whether they have ever been systematized in so complex a design as that which lies in Somerset, it is quite certain no other earth effigies have such a mass of legend associated with them.

Consequently the following notes are not concerned with the Grail of the Christian era, but with an earlier "Grail," that "Cauldron of Wisdom" already famous ages before Joseph of Arimathea brought his message here. It was, no doubt, the very reason for his choice of so remote a spot, for it is a matter of history that Christianity came to Glastonbury prior to any other place in the British Isles. Dugdale in his Monasticon, commenting on the Druids in no measured terms, writes: "About sixty-three years after the incarnation of our Lord, St. Joseph of Arimathea, accompanied by eleven other disciples of St. Philip, was despatched by that apostle into Britain to introduce the meek and gentle system of Christianity . . . they settled in the Isle of Avilion."

Nevertheless, even after that event, the neighbourhood continued to be haunted by giants, a lion, and "many other things," part of the legend heritage that had gathered about this land chart of the sky. The following chapters not only describe each astronomical giant as it lies prone upon the ground, but draws attention to the manner in which the Grail History refers to it: we have at last three definite sources of information besides the Arthurian legends, viz.: the Ordnance Survey large scale maps, the pictured astronomical figures of our present globes, and photographs taken from the air.

It might be supposed that one could see such creatures on any map! but it would be impossible to find a **circular** traditional design of Zodiacal and other constellation figures, arranged in their proper order, and corresponding **with their respective stars,** unless they had thus been laid out in sequence, according to plan. Nor could one find thirteen heads designedly turned towards the sunset, with their bodies turning round a Central Point on which they all pivot! Their drawing is proportionally fine.

The text here used is **The High History of the Holy Graal** in its English translation by Dr. Sabastian Evans, it is from the French version **Perceval le Gallois ou le conte du Graal;** "nearly one-seventh of the whole of a copy in handwriting of the thirteenth century is preserved" writes Dr. Evans in giving a full account of the manuscript.

The name of the author is not known; that he was well acquainted with the Sea Moors of Somerset is now apparent from his accurate know-

2

ledge of the effigy giants; in fact they never would have been found had it not been for the guidance of this **History.**

On the last page of the **High History** we read: "The Latin from whence this History was drawn into Romance, was taken in the Isle of Avalon, in a holy house of religion that standeth at the head of the Moors Adventurous, there where King Arthur and Queen Guenievre lie," for the King is one of those giant Cosmic Deities, upon which every pilgrim who climbs Glastonbury Tor looks down, but can no longer distinguish.

The author of another version, called **La Queste del Saint Graal,** though apparently not familiar with the locality, is more explicit concerning the adaptation of the old stellar religion to the new: for instance he says: "When the sun, by which we mean Jesus Christ," and again, in Sir Lancelot's dream, he speaks of "the man all surrounded by stars," and the man who came down from heaven, came to the younger knight and "transformed him into the figure of a lion and gave him wings." Here is strongly suggested the blending of old and new, the Zodiacal Leo combined with the winged Lion of St. Mark.

Thus the pre-Christian stories of the stars were adapted by the later chroniclers and interwoven with the Christian Grail legend.

> "The old order changeth, yielding place to new,
> And God fulfils Himself in many ways,
> Lest one good custom should corrupt the world,"

as the King says in Tennyson's **Passing of Arthur,** when his funeral barge disappeared in "the island-valley of Avilion."

But as foretold, King Arthur, the Sun King, will come again; he shines as Hercules in the night sky, reflected in his sleeping effigy on the "Moors Adventurous." Those who had been initiated into the mysteries of this "island valley" were obliged to couch their secret knowledge in romance, after Christianity swept the field; but neither that reformation, nor any other, was able to destroy the map of the stars that our forefathers modelled amongst the hills and river beds of Somerset, and which still testifies to the ancient religion of this land; Dr. L. A. Waddell suggests that it was brought here by the Early Phœnician sun and star worshippers 2800 B.C. (see **Phœnician Origin of Britons).**

Speaking of the Phœnicians Mr. J. S. M. Ward quotes from "The Leyland-Locke MS." in his **Outline History of Freemasonry:**

3

"Pythagoras, a Grecian, travelled to acquire knowledge in Egypt and Syria and in every land where the Phœnicians had planted Freemasonry." If they did so, these ancient landmarks should reveal more than one lost secret. Fortunately there is no necessity to excavate in order to reveal "the imitation of the Divine plan (in Somerset) that was designed to account for the return of the Seasons," for it lies on the surface as long as the Zodiacal Giants retain their "beautiful proportions."

William of Malmesbury's expression: "A Heavenly Sanctuary on Earth," where lies King Arthur, might certainly be taken to mean the constellations laid out on Earth, one of which represents King Arthur, for literally this is true. The pre-Christian Temple there, was that of the hills and rivers, adapted in such a way as to resemble the Dome of Heaven inverted on Earth.

To understand, one has to study the traditional picture of the northern hemisphere which astronomers have fortunately preserved, and visualise it laid out on the earth, like an enormous garden—it is called in the **High History** the garden of Eden—and there is the setting of the Arthurian drama, the "System of the Round Table."

The **High History** says: "Never was the chapel wasted nor decayed, but was as whole thereafter as tofore and is so still." Branch 35. Title 27.)

"I saw the Graal, saith the Master, or ever Joseph collected therein the blood of Jesus Christ." (Branch 35. Title 7.)

"The history witnesseth us that in the land of King Arthur at this time was there not a single chalice. The Graal appeared at the sacring of the mass, in five several manners that none ought not to tell, for the secret things of the sacrament ought none to tell openly, but he unto whom God hath given it. King Arthur beheld all the changes, the last whereof was the change into a chalice." (Branch 22. Title3.)

Thus, the Christian's Grail in which "the blood of Jesus Christ was collected" took the place of an earlier and far vaster conception, to which Christian tradition naturally lays no claim, as the late Dean of Wells pointed out in **Two Glastonbury Legends**: "Be that as it may, the fact remains that the Glastonbury tradition to the very end, though it borrowed what it wanted from 'the book which is called **The Holy Grail**,' makes no claim, no allusion even, to the Grail itself."

To quote Spence's **Encyclopædia**: "This world being unworthy, the Graal was said to be removed, yet not hidden, **for it is always discernible**

4

by any one worthy or qualified to see it"; and though the Romance, **Perceval le Gallois**, which that artist Sebastian Evans translated into such quaint English, casts a mediæval veil over the pre-Christian Celestial Temple of the Mysteries, it is possible, with careful study, to reconstruct it from that text by aid of modern maps.

Plutarch must have had something of the kind in his mind when he wrote of Britain. "Moreover there is, they said, an island in which Cronus is imprisoned, with Briareus keeping guard over him as he sleeps; for, as they put it, sleep is the bond forged for Cronus. They add that around him are many divinities, his henchmen and attendants." **(Didot Edition of Plutarch, Vol. 3, Page 511.)**

To realise at all the magnitude of the prehistoric "Round Table of the Grail," one is obliged to think in miles instead of inches, in thousands of years instead of hundreds; for the Temple is ten miles in diameter, it is about 5,000 years old, and this counterpart of the heavens, corresponds with the constellation figures recognized by astronomers today.

It is interesting to note in passing, that it was once customary to personify the heavenly bodies and elements in religious drama and dance; "one of the favourite mysteries presented by strolling companies in the southern provinces of China" is called The Spectacle of the Sun and Moon. (Wright, **China.**) That is exactly what the pre-Christian Grail "Mystery" appears to have been, three knights and King Arthur representing the sun in the four Quarters of the years, within the "Golden Round," each having his own "house" or constellation Giant. What is so extraordinarily interesting, is the fact that the **High History** makes them perform on their original Giant stage in Somerset, where their effigies have been lying for thousands of years.

No doubt our star-gazing ancestors thought by sympathetic magic to realise Heaven on Earth, when they fashioned, what Homer in the 11th Book of the **Odyssey** might have described as a "wondrous zone" . . . "where woodland monsters grin" . . . "inimitably wrought with skill divine."

Robert Brown says in **Primitive Constellations:** "The Greeks received the constellation names and nearly all the stories connected with them, not from any savages, but from the highly civilized Phœnicians, who in turn, like the ancient Arabians, had obtained many of these names from the archaic civilization of the Euphrates Valley, whose chart of the heavens had been already completed B.C. 2084."

It is difficult for us to realise that all over India and in many other parts of the world, the stars are still being worshipped, as they were here before St. Joseph came.

The ancient Javanese signs of the Zodiac surrounded by gods of agriculture, seen on their zodiacal cups, resemble the Somerset ones very closely; and their World Tree motive, belonging to the oldest Asiatic civilization, shows a lion, bull, birds and snake all up in the branches of this Tree of Life, with a giant, griffins and dwarfs below. **The High History of the Holy Graal** is not only written in the form of a tree with thirty-five branches, but contains these celestial creatures within the branches, and includes griffins, giants and dwarfs.

The reason why we are still able to trace the Zodiacal creatures, is that the land on which they lie was once the property of "the first church in Britain," and up to the time of the Reformation the monks of Glastonbury were scrupulously careful to keep the ancient landmarks and waterways intact; doubtless "They had the whole History thereof true from the beginning even to the end," as the **High History** tells us. The learned Dean of Wells remarked in **Two Glastonbury Legends**:

"But as the tales in connection with which the Grail first makes its appearance are Celtic tales, it is now generally believed that the Grail itself has its prototype in the mystic cauldron of unfailing supply and the magic cup of healing, which are also elements of Celtic mythology."

> "Avalon's island, with avidity
> Claiming the death of pagans,
> More than all in the world beside,
> For the entombment of them all,
> Honoured by **chanting spheres of prophecy**:
> And for all time to come
> Adorned shall it be
> By them that praise the Highest."

Melkin, the British Bard.

As a preliminary to tracing the wanderings of the Knights of King Arthur over the tracks and along the streams that outline their Giant Effigies, it will be useful to consult Bartholomew's half-inch to the mile map, Sheet 34. That excellent map, though on too small a scale to show all the giants in detail, gives a general idea of the little island, "Kingdom of Logres," as it is called in the Grail History, surrounded by its green

Sea Moors. There we shall find, if we look closely, Leo outlined by the Cary river and two of its streams between Copley Wood and Lytes Cary; and the Giant Orion sitting near it formed by the two Dundon Hills.

Alfred's Fort at Athelney and Camelot Castle at South Cadbury, are both eleven miles from the Isle of Avalon.

By noting the places within this area where the Knights appear to meet one another, and knowing the time it would take to ride there from the last encounter, it is possible gradually to make a complete itinerary and map of the Quest—disregarding, of course, fabulous distances which obviously refer to the starry sky. Such a map to The **High History of the Holy Graal** was made by me in 1929, and published by Dent in the Everyman's Library; up till then no suggestion apparently of a Zodiacal Round Table of the Grail had been put forward, despite innumerable theories, and The Kingdom of Logres had not been located; see Plate 7, in which the Lion, Giant Twin, Bull's head, Ram and Fish have already been indicated.

7

THE CHIEF CHARACTERS OF "THE HIGH HISTORY OF THE HOLY GRAAL," AND WHAT THEY STAND FOR

1. (Earth) Taurus — **King Gurgalain.**
2. (Fire) Aries — **Messire Gawain**=The Sun in the second Quarter.
3. (Water) Pisces — **King Fisherman.**
4. (Air) Aquarius — **King Pelles,** succeeded by **Sir Perceval**=The Sun in the first Quarter of the year, represented by the Phœnix.
5. (Earth) Capricornus — **King of Castle Mortal.**
6. (Fire) Sagittarius and Hercules — **King Arthur**=The Sun in the east; and the last Quarter of the year.
7. (Water) Scorpio and — **Calixtus,** whose soul is weighed (in the Scales of death).
8. (Air) Libra
9. (Earth) Virgo — **The Damsel,** Sir Perceval's sister, also called **Dindrain.**
10. (Fire) Leo and — **Sir Lancelot of the Lake**=The Midday Sun in the south; and the third Quarter of the year.
11. (Water) Cancer
12. (Air) Gemini — **Lohot,** King Arthur's son=The Sun in west, the Setting Sun; represented by the "Giant" Orion in effigy.

Sir Perceval=The spirit of the Sun after it has set, represented by the Bird on the rudder of Orion's Ship.

13. Canis Minor — **Meliot of Logres.**
14. Cetus — **Gohaz of the Castle of the Whale.**
15. Draco — **The Black Knight, the Giant Devil.**
16. Hydra — **Queen Guenievre.**

The Great Hound, of the Parrett River, is **the wife of Marin the Jealous of Little Gomerit.**

THE EARTH CHART OF THE STARS IN SOMERSET

The following list shows how the stars fall in regard to their corresponding Nature Effigies.

To prove the correspondence of the Earth Giants with the celestial constellations as they are depicted by astronomers to-day, lay Philips' Planisphere—which is the same size—on the back of the accompanying effigy chart of the heavens—frontispiece—and prick the stars through. If the square of Ursa Minor be laid on the "giant dragon's" head, at the centre of the circle; with Aldebaran on the Equinoctial line to the west, and Antares on the same line to the east; then the rest of the stars will fall as stated below; they are thus shown on Plate 2.

THE LION
Because of its great size, the effigy Leo includes the whole of the constellation Cancer in his neck, as well as Castor and Pollux from Gemini on his mask. Also the head of Hydra is contained within his body. Leo's Royal Star Regulus and all his "Sickle" stars fall around his tail which hangs over his back.

THE VIRGIN
Zavijava and the stars of Virgo near it, with Denebola from Leo, fall around her Sheaf of Wheat the 'Kern-baby.' Spica falls on her skirt.

THE SCORPION
Zubeneschamali and Zubenel-genubi from Libra fall in the right claw, which here takes the place of the Scales. Stars of Lupus and Serpens are contained within the effigy. The Royal Star Antares and the five other Scorpion stars near it marked the centre of its body on the Fosse Way.

THE ARCHER
HERCULES
These two constellations are here combined to form a centaur. All the greater stars of Sagittarius fall in the hind quarters of the horse. On its chest fall Altair, Tarazed and Alschain from Aquila, the rest of that constellation stretching across the shoulders of the horse.
Practically the whole constellation of Hercules corresponds with his earth counterpart; whilst all the stars of Lyra fall on his back. Eltanin and other Draco stars fall on his right arm.

9

THE GOAT	Prima Giedi, Dabih and the greater part of Capricornus correspond with the goat; whilst Equuleus falls in the head.
THE WATER BEARER	This constellation is represented by the Phoenix, drinking from Chalice Blood Spring. Sadal Melik, Skat and several other stars of Aquarius correspond with the wings of the bird effigy, whilst Markab from Pegasus falls by its very interesting crest, formed of cultivation terraces called Chapels.
THE FISHES	Three of the stars that in the sky connect Pisces, fall respectively on the tail of the Whale, on one of the Fishes, and on the road connecting them.
THE RAM	The whole of the constellation Aries falls on the neck of the effigy, the head being reverted towards the west.
THE BULL	The Royal Star Aldebaran falls on the "bell" under the Bull's dewlap. The Hyades fall on the right fore-leg. The Pleiades fall on the neck of Taurus. Capella in Auriga, falls just below the tip of the horns, which are marked by earthworks along Hatch Hill.

ORION THE GIANT	This takes the place of one of the Twins, two stars from Gemini falling on his uplifted right hand. Betelgeuze, Rigel, Bellatrix, Mintaka, Anilam, in fact all the stars of Orion correspond, except the Lion's skin. Nath and the other horn star from Taurus, fall on his elbow and head.
THE HARE	The stars of Lepus fall on the seat and high poop of the Ship, in which Orion is sitting cross-legged, sailing along the river of stars Eridanus.
CANIS MAJOR (not shown on Plate 1)	The place of this constellation is taken by a "Griffon" bird that faces Orion. Sirius, Murzim, in fact all the stars of Canis Major fall within the boundary of this Hawk-headed bird, whose tail lies between the paws of the Lion and flows over his ribs. The central stars of Monoceros fall along its back.

URSA MAJOR	The place of this constellation is taken by a third and smaller bird. The wing pointing west corresponds with Benetnasch, Mizar, Alioth and Megrez.
CANIS MINOR	The place of this constellation is taken by the head of a Dog at Littleton; the hill forming it being supplemented by mounds and an ancient trackway along the top; it is surrounded by the sites of Roman Villas. Gomeisa falls on the neck, by the Lion's raised right paw.
URSA MINOR	The place of this constellation is taken by the head of Draco. The ancient Pole Star Kochab falls on it. It lies in the "Crown of the Land."

THE GREAT DOG	of the Parrett River, has no corresponding stars, as it lies outside the Circle of Cosmic giants, guarding the tidal entrance to the "Kingdom of Logres."

It is remarkable that the stars which agree with their corresponding constellation figures on the ground, only lie along the celestial path of the sun, moon and planets; with the notable exception of the Giants Hercules and Orion, whose stars also fit their correct effigies, when transferred from the modern planisphere on to the map of Somerset.

"TABULA SMARAGDINA"

"Heaven above, Heaven below;
Stars above, Stars below;
All that is over, under shall show.
Happy thou who the riddle readest."

Quoted by Dmitri Merejkowski in **The Forerunner.**

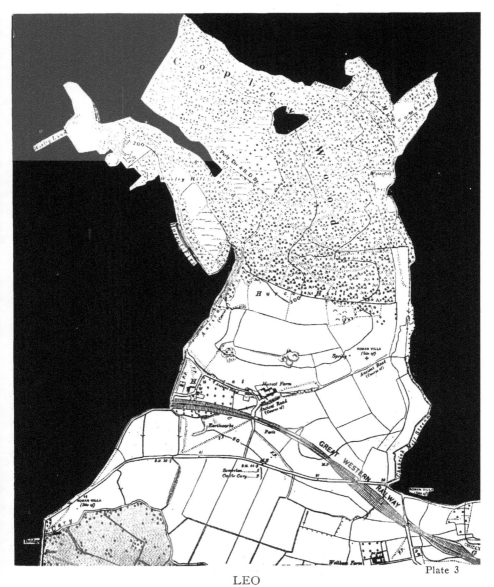

Plate 3

LEO

Chabrick Mill Stream outlines the nose and mane, "Ancient Road" the neck, and "Linches" the jaw.

13

THE GREAT SECRETS

"If ye are primitive Bards,
According to the discipline of qualified instructors,
Relate the great secrets
Of the world which we inhabit."—

"There is a formidable animal,
From the City of Satanas,
Which has made an inroad
Between the deep and the shallows.
His mouth is as wide
As the mountains of Mynnau:
Neither death can vanquish him,
Nor hand, nor sword.
There is a load of nine hundred rocks
Between his two paws:
There is one eye in his head,
Vivid as the blue ice."

Taliesin the Bard.

* * *

"Their swords broke and bounded off from him as if they were struck upon an anvil." "So they took off his hair shirt" . . . "he smiled and replied, 'this fire can not so much as singe my hair.'"

La Queste del Sainte Graal, page 97.
W. W. Comfort's translation.

CHAPTER I

THE FIRE SIGN, LEO
THE LION OF THE "FORBIDDEN LAND" OF LOGRES

JULY and AUGUST

The High History of the Holy Graal. Branch 9. Title 3.

"'We wait,' saith the Mistress of the damsels, 'some knight that shall clear this pass, for no knight durst pass hereby.' 'What is the pass, then, damsel?' saith he. 'It is the one of a lion, and a lion, moreover, so fell and horrible that never was none seen more cruel.' . . .

. . . Clamados looketh and seeth the hall within an enclosure and seeth the lion that lay at the entrance of the gateway. As soon as he espieth Clamados and the damsels, he cometh toward them full speed, mouth open and ears pricked up."

The boundaries of "the Field of the Lion" are as follows. The ribs and front part of the hind leg and foot are outlined by the Cary River; the nose, mane and tail, by streams that flow into it. The back, throat and front legs by 'ancient' roads. The jaw is modelled by earthworks called 'Linches' on the map.

"From the Time of the Coming of Brutus"

John of Glaston tells us that King Arthur's armorial bearings were three red lions: "His arms also he changed in their honour, for they were silver, with three lions red, turning their heads to their backs, from the time of the coming of Brutus even unto this change."

Geoffrey of Monmouth says that this Brutus or "Brute the first King of the Britons," was a Trojan; now the Trojan War was about 1184 B.C., so according to these statements the Brutus lion may have been the original of the hereditary arms of our kings and queens, two thousand years and more before Richard I. is said to have brought the heraldic lion from Asia Minor.

Astrologically, Bristol, Bath and Taunton, all within thirty miles of the effigy, are 'reigned over' by Leo, as W. T. Olcott says in **Star Lore of All Ages.**

15

BRUT D'ANGLETTERE

"From Noe unto Eneas,
And what betwixt tham was.
And fro Eneas till Brutus tyme,
That kynde he tells in this ryme.
Fro Brutus to Cadweladres,
The last Briton that this land lees,
Alle that kynd and alle the fruit
That came of Brutus that is the Brute;
And the ryght Brut is told no more.
Than the Brytons tyme wore.
After the Bretons the Inglis camen,
The lordchip of this land thai namen."

Robert de Brunne's translation from the
Roman de Brut of Wace, C. 1124-1174.

The Arthurian Lion a Nature Effigy

The lion is an integral part of Arthurian romance; for instance, in the story of **Owein and Lunet** it kills the man-eating giant, and is also associated with the ring and the serpent. In **The High History of the Holy Graal** it is several times represented as being killed by Arthur's knights, but like the giants lives to fight another day.

Though it has long since been recognized as the lion of Light, it is obviously intended to be something more tangible as well, for in **Peredur,** "a lion, bound with a chain, asleep by the side of a rock," suggests a sculptural or heraldic beast; the romance goes on to say that the giant remarked concerning it: "Shame on my gate-keeper's beard." (We shall come to the chain and beard later.)

So it was whilst pondering on the characteristics of this fabulous creature, with Bartholomew's map, Sheet 34, open before me, that the Cary river was seen to take the outline of a lion, with the ancient capital of Somerset "a load of nine hundred rocks between his two paws."

That was the first realization of the possibility that, if the lion were indeed a nature effigy, then the giant must be another close by! and it was only later that 'the lion of the Zodiac' was suggested.

Other Constellation Effigies Outlined

Many years of questing on that trail, proved that a Romano-British road from Ilchester, which crosses the Cary at Somerton Erleigh on the Lion's chest, outlines the Giant Orion's raised forearm; the Bull's lower jaw; the Ram's bent knee, neck and head; and goes over the bridges connecting the Whale and the Fishes at Street. This road then outlines one of the Fishes; part of the tail and head of the Glastonbury Phœnix; the top of the head of the Goatfish; the two legs of Hercules that straddle the withers of The Archer's horse; and the tail of the Scorpion as far as Stone on the Fosse Way. Now, facing south-west, the Roman road makes a short cut through the centre of the Scorpion's body and its right claw, passing close by the place of the star Spica on the Virgin's robe, to skirt her hand; then the older road outlines her Wheatsheaf and the back and shoulder of the Lion, joining the Somerton Erleigh track once more.

In this way a devotee could ride from one constellation effigy to another, in contact with the path of the sun, without leaving the beaten track, which is now a motor road.

But, to reduce the ride to a distance of twenty miles, the pilgrim could leave out the Scorpion of death, and follow up the body of Hercules 'The King' to Baltonsborough, crossing Tootle Bridge to join the Virgin's Wheatsheaf road by Keinton Mandeville; the route, shown on Plate 7 of The Kingdom of Logres, passes along the inner outline of ten effigy constellations; this amazing piece of draughtsmanship, without further demonstration, is enough to prove the skill of the design.

At the centre of the interesting shape thus formed is the effigy Finger, that lies on the supposed Equinoctial Line of this Nature Temple, and points to Taurus.

Somerton, the Former Capital

The Romanized Britons of Somerton did not surrender to the Saxons till A.D. 733; so it is not surprising that many place-names in this particular neighbourhood are of pagan origin.

In the seventh century the town was walled, and drew its water supply from Ringer's Well, to which the closed up archway in the cellar of the ruined castle may have given access. Ringer's Well, now disused, is said to have had five springs in a ring: they rose by Sun House Farm just west of the old castle site, at present occupied by the White Hart Inn.

To the east of this was King Ina's palace, probably on the site of a much earlier village.

The Tithe Barn and Old Parsonage are also on the south east of the

17

present town, whilst to the west the Lion's left paw lay on Maypole Knap.

Of course there is a Red Lion Inn at Somerton, and, though there are some interesting old houses, it is in the Church of St. Michael that the visitor will linger, gazing at the roof with its four splendid dragons repeated five times. It is of the thirteenth century, carved by the monks of Muchelney Island near Langport, but redolent of early traditions concerning mythical beasts.

The High History of the Holy Graal. Branch 24. Titles 6 and 7.

"there is therein a lion, the fiercest and most horrible in the world, and two serpents that are called griffons, that have the face of a man and the beaks of birds and eyes of an owl and teeth of a dog and ears of an ass and feet of a lion and tail of a serpent, and they have couched them therewithin, but never saw no man beasts so fell and felonous."

"So soon as they heard him coming they dress them on their feet, and then writhe along as serpents, then cast forth such fire, and so bright a flame amidst the rock, as that all the cavern is lighted up thereof, and they see by the brightness of light of their jaws the brachet coming."

Whilst repairing the church roof, balls were found lodged in it.

The following is from an article by Mr. H. J. Massingham, "How Ball Games began," published in the **Listener,** August 3rd, 1932:

"The game was not a sport but a religious service." . . . "The ball game was played by peoples with a social organisation which was split into two halves for ritual purposes: one side of the community representing the sky-world and its solar cult, and the other the under-world." At Dorking in Surrey the traditional ball game was played once a year on Shrove Tuesday, and the players came from the east and west sides of the church. Their costumes represented some of "the ancient king gods of Briton."

The altar table in St. Michael's Church, dated 1626, tells the story of the prehistoric Grail; for the High History calls the Grail Castle, Eden.

The carving on the right leg shows the Cup standing on a book, which is supported by an hour-glass at rest; the hands of God have closed (or are about to open) this volume of Time.

18

The next leg shows Adam and Eve sitting under the Tree, round the trunk of which coils the inevitable Draco.

On the third, Adam delves and ploughs the ridged fields with a primitive hand plough.

In front, on the fourth leg of the table, Noah is building the Ark above his head, by aid of a conspicuously placed Mason's Square; his right hand chops the wood with a large hatchet.

From the Left Fore Paw to the Hind Leg

Not far from Somerton, lying in the hind quarters of the Lion, is the village of Charlton Mackrell. The church has an interesting wood carving on a bench end, representing a Satyr holding a scroll in each claw, one scroll closed and the other unfurled, a sack hangs over his shoulder, at his side a flower grows out of a great book, in his stomach is a face. This pantheistic figure has some connection with the first zodiacal Grail, for there is 'a miniature of the Holy Graal' in a fifteenth century MS. in the Bibliotheque Nationale, Paris, showing a composite being not unlike this one, in its attempt to portray the Cosmos by combining stellar symbols. The head has three faces with three horns; a suggestion of two dragon's heads on the shoulders, and clawed feet; it holds a bull's head—Taurus— on the top of a wand, and has four faces on its shoulders and knees representing the four quarters of the heavens, and a fifth great bearded face on the stomach, which face symbolizes the fertilizing sun. On a house in the main street at Wivelscombe, Somerset, there is a carving of Adam with this face on his stomach: on the same house other interesting subjects are depicted such as Eve nursing a great serpent. Some years ago at a fancy dress ball on board a Japanese ship, two stewards appeared with faces painted on the same part of their anatomy; no one seemed to think it unusual, and presumably they represented the sun and moon.

And now to return to the topographical details of Logres, for that is the name of the Kingdom of the Quest of the Holy Grail.

An Alabaster Quarry on the Lion's Collar

From Sometron to Charlton Mackrell station, the G.W.R. line makes a double curve through the entire length of the lion. On the hill to the north of the railway is the white alabaster quarry which once adorned his collar but is now covered with moss and grass. The name Hurcot for the quarry hill is suggestive of the Celtic sun god, Hu: we find it again in Huish Road, which outlines the lower part of the lion's body. Because

19

of his great size, the effigy Leo includes the stars of the constellation Cancer.

The Lion's Ears

Romano-British villas lay to the south and north of the railway line: one of them is marked by a heap of stones in the Lion's left ear, now completely overgrown with trees; it is still called Magotty Pagotty, or mother god father god, thus echoing the prayers that were whispered into the ear of this "woodland monster."

Cedar Walk avenue curves round from near Kingweston Church, through Staddlecombe Plantation, to a tall sun-dial on top of the rounded hill that forms the right "pricked ear;" this hill was also approached by a farm track through a cutting that led to the Troughs of the Twelve Apostles, as they are called locally. The twelve Troughs are about 14 in. wide, 7 in. deep, and 3 ft., more or less, long, made of slabs of stone descending in shallow steps, through which a never failing spring flows on into Charbrick Mill Stream. This stream forms an incrustation of calcium carbonate on whatever it passes over, the fantastic shapes thus made no doubt invested the water with supposedly supernatural powers, once upon a time.

The Enchanted Springs of Logres

Three other springs of like nature belong to the Kingdom of Logres; one flows out of Pocock's Cave; another is in the body of the Sagittarius horse effigy on the south side of Pennard Hill, where its stones are called Washing Stones; a third spring which has the same fantastic habit is in what I shall call the Enclosure of the Sun at Butleigh. Here follows the analysis of the water from the spring that used to flow out of Pocock's Cave at Ford Farm, Chilton Polden: the entrance to the cave fell in a hundred years ago and the stream was diverted to a tunnel near by:

	Grains per gallon
Silica SiO_2 - - - - - - - - -	Traces
Ferric Oxide Fe_2O_3 - - - - - -	Traces
Alumina Al_2O_3 - - - - - - -	Traces
Calcium Sulphate $CaSO_4$ - - - - -	102.0
Calcium Carbonate $CaCO_3$ - - - - -	24.0
Magnesium Sulphate $MgSO_4$ - - - -	23.0
Total Chlorides equal to Sodium Chloride $NaCl$	4.0
Total Nitrates equal to Sodium Nitrate $NaNO_3$	0.2
Carbonic Acid (Anhydride) CO_2 - more than	11.0

Leo is Personified by Lancelot

In the Introduction we pointed out that King Arthur and his Knights personify the effigy constellation figures though called by other names; thus in Branch 7. Titles 1, 2 and 3, of the **High History** we find Sir Lancelot of the Lake, who personifies Leo, in company with one of the Twins—Gemini—the other Twin having been slain "of succouring" him, Lancelot is making much of the remaining one. The Explanation of this may be that when the stars Castor and Pollux are transferred from the celestial planisphere to the'map, the star Pollux falls in the mouth of the Lion, and the star Castor by his nose.

Sir Lancelot, having killed the Lord of the Rock Gladoens and given it back to the surviving Twin, might be said to 'beard the lion in his den' at "the Castle of Beards." Now as regards beards the following 'giant' story is told by J. Rhys in **Celtic Folk Lore.**

A Mantle Made of Beards

Nynio and Peibio were brothers: one moonlight night Nynio said 'See, what a fine extensive field I possess, the whole firmament.' Peibio answered that 'the whole host of stars' with 'the moon shepherding them' belonged to him; over which statement they fought a war of extermination. The Giant Rhita conquered Nynio and Peibio and shaved off their beards, and the beards of many Kings. With these beards he made a mantle to 'cover him from head to foot.' He was probably this lion of the Castle of Beards. Geoffrey of Monmouth says that the Giant asked Arthur for his beard to fix above the others; and the **High History** tells us:

Branch 7. Titles 4 and 5.

" 'It is the pass of the Castle of Beards, and it hath the name of this, that every knight that passeth thereby must either leave his beard there or challenge the same, and in such sort have I challenged my beard that meseemeth I shall die thereof.' 'By my head,' saith Lancelot, 'I hold not this of cowardize, sith that you were hardy to set your life in jeopardy to challenge your beard, but now would you argue me of cowardize when you would have me turn back. Rather would I be smitten through the body with honour, so and I had not my death thereof, than lose with shame a single hair of my beard.' 'Sir,' saith the knight, 'May God preserve you, for the castle is far more cruel than you think.' "

"Lancelot looketh at the gateway of the castle and seeth the great door all covered with beards fastened thereon, and heads of knights in great plenty hung thereby. So, as he was about to enter the gate, two knights issue therefrom over against him. 'Sir,' saith the one, 'Abide and pay your toll!' 'Do knights, then, pay toll here?' saith Lancelot. 'Yea!' say the knights, 'All they that have beards, and they that have none are quit. Sir, now pay us yours, for a right great beard it is, and thereof have we sore need.' 'For what?' saith Lancelot. 'I will tell you,' saith the knight. 'There be hermits in this forest that make hair-shirts thereof.' 'But my head,' saith Lancelot, 'Never shall they have hair-shirt of mine.' "

The Grave-Yard Perilous Lies Either Side of the Lion's Tail

Then follows a horrid repast obviously served by the victims the lion has mauled.

Sir Lancelot now goes to the lion's tail, by the "tall cross," (Christian's Cross) of the "Grave-yard Perilous;" Leo's Royal Star Regulus falls near it on Boxhill; this star must have been of special importance to star worshippers, for Regulus is in the path of the moon as well as the sun; it was occulted by the moon on April 6th, 1933.

If Bartholomew's map Sheet 34 be consulted, it will be seen that though Christian's Cross lies on comparatively low ground, it commands an extensive view towards the east of the surrounding Wiltshire and Dorsetshire hills : the pre-historic castle of Camelot, at South Cadbury, seven miles away, can be distinguished by its great clump of trees, and beside it the perfectly bare round hill, Par Rock, to be described later with Camelot.

The lion's tail is outlined by a Brook—not shown on Bartholomew's map—that commencing at the Cross curves round over the back in the shape of Leo's 'Sickle,' towards Charlton House, where it joins the body of the creature; it is then made to outline its rump and flows on into the Cary river.

On the corner of Boxhill Lane and the road descending Snap Hill, is a circular pond made by laying wrought stones in diminishing circles; a stream from a spring runs through it : there is a similar pond just north of Christian's Cross in Kingweston Park that is more than two hundred feet in circumference.

22

Somerton Lane Is Not A Motor Road

The whole of the back of the lion is outlined by an ancient road called Somerton Lane, running from the site of a Roman Villa, near the railway arch at the bottom of Snap Hill, to Charlton House, where it meets the brook which forms the tail. From here the road coming from Christian's Cross draws the hind quarters and leg as far as Cary Bridge near Lyte's Cary.

Either side of the hind foot are sites of so-called Roman Villas: Holly Hill Lane leads to one from Kingsdon.

The river from Cary Bridge draws the front of the hind leg as it flows north and west to the 'lion waist,' then the ribs as it flows west, to pass under the second Cary Bridge on the chest: the Lion—about three miles long—lies exactly between these two bridges of the same name.

The Lion's Head

Copley House is near the tip of his nose, where Chabrick Mill Stream rises: Copley Wood covers the whole of the top of the head, and Long Wood forms his "open" mouth, whilst Worley Hill and Hurcot Firs and Linches model his lower jaw.

In early November on a sunny day, the hanging woods here are a riot of colour, below them lies the red tongue of the Lion, outlined by a footpath shown on Plate 3; it points to the Giant Orion.

The "right great beard" mentioned in Branch 7. Title 5, is formed of red marl and hangs down between Worley Lane and Worley Hill. This name suggests that the whirls or customary 'wheels of fire' were rolled down from this hill at the solstitial fire festival.

It might have been possible to see the whole of the Lion from Somerton Wood—where there was a Tumulus, now destroyed,—for it is high above Somerton Erleigh, but the beech trees are so fine they completely hide the view for the greater part of the year.

Castley Hill forms his right front paw: from here the valley of the Cary river can be seen, and also the charming semi-circular escarpment showing the Rhaetic Beds that bound King's Sedge Moor and form the isolated Dundon Hills. Owlsley lies in the deep hollow behind the angle of the flat jaw bone; on the edge of this hollow the map marks 'track of ancient road,' which runs down to the site of a Romano-British Villa by Cary Bridge, thus outlining the throat and chest bone.

23

Leo Lies In Catsash Hundred

This Leo may have been 'Pa Lug's Cat,' the cat of the god of light, and the cat that the Knights Templars were said to worship, for it lies partly in Catsash Hundred.

Colonel Waddell says in his **Phœnician Origin of Britons and Scots,** page 208:

"Catti was the title of the earliest British Kings," and "From Somerton in the Severn Valley we find a series of early 'Catti' names radiating through Cambria or Wales to some extent. The very free distribution of this Catti and Barat title in Somerset, or 'Seat of the Somers,' with its relative absence in Wales and mainly confined there to the Severn Coast, suggests that Somerset, with the northern bank of the Severn estuary, from Caerleon or Isca on the Usk, to Gower, formed the Cymry Land."

It is noticeable that the chief Druid of Britain was called 'a Lion.' William Olcott tells us in **Star Lore of All Ages:** "Leo is for many reasons significant to Masons. In the four Royal Stars, the four great Elohim, or Decans, gods ruling the signs were believed to dwell. The four Decans who ruled the four angles of the heavens were the most important and most powerful. To these four Stars divine honours were paid, and sacred images were erected in which the Lion, Eagle, Ox and Man were variously combined. These figures appear on the Royal Arch Banner."

Four stars are shown in a row on the left-hand side of Christ in the tympanum over the south door of the church at Moissac, the date of the carving is 1063 (see photo in **Romanesque France,** by V. Markham).

"Miracles Should Not Cease Till the Great Lion Had Come"

One of the most interesting references to the Somerset Lion is a very ancient note in William of Malmesbury's **Antiquities of Glastonbury** (F. Lomax's translation, published by Talbot), which says: "that miracles should not cease until the great lion had come, having a tail fastened with great chains. Again, in what follows concerning the search for a cup which is there called the Holy Graal, the same is related almost at the beginning." That was in connection with Lancelot du Lac of the Round Table, for whom his comrades were searching.

The reason why King Arthur imprisoned his best knight Lancelot must be that he was acting the part of this Lion, for however brave Leo's Summer sun, Arthur's Autumnal decree is inevitable.

Branch 30. Title 21.

"'You come hither for another thing," saith the King, 'according to that I have been given to wit, and, had the hall been void of folk, you hoped to have slain me.' The King commandeth him be taken forthwith without gainsay of any."

However Arthur relents and has him brought out of "his dungeon in the prison."

Branch 34. Titles 2 and 3.

"He made bring Lancelot before him into the midst of the hall, that was somewhat made lean of his being in prison."

Leo's burning "manor" is vividly described in Branch 20. Title 2, where Lancelot "felt the men that lay dead, and groped among them from head to head and felt that there was a great heap of them there, and came back and sate at the fire all laughing." Such savage mirth savours again of a lion!

Those **chains** fastening the pagan lion's **tail** must be Christian's Cross which is the name of the crossroads on his tail before pointed out, but the stars of Leo's 'Sickle' are what originally fastened his upturned tail to the zodiacal Path.

Branch 15. Title 14 to 18.

"The cross was at the entrance of the grave-yard, that was right spacious, for, from such time as the land was first peopled of folk, and that knights began to seek adventure by the forest, not a knight had died in the forest, that was full great of breadth and length, but his body was borne thither."

"The damsel beholdeth their sepulchres all round about the grave-yard whereinto she was come. She seeth them surrounded of knights, all black, and spears had they withal, and came one against another, and made such uproar and alarm as it seemed all the forest resounded thereof. The most part held swords all red as fire . . . She seeth above the altar the most holy cloth for the which she was come thither,

25

that was right ancient, and a smell came thereof so sweet and glorious that no sweetness of the world might equal it. The damsel cometh toward the altar thinking to take the cloth, but it goeth up into the air as if the wind had lifted it . . . Forthwith the cloth came down above the altar, and she straighway found taken away therefrom as much as it pleased Our Lord she should have. Josephus telleth us of a truth, that never did none enter the chapel that might touch the cloth save only this one damsel."

The cloth that "goeth up into the air as if the wind had lifted it," must be the tuft on the end of the lion's tail, for the Damsel is Virgo of the Cary river into which the Brook outlining the tail flows, after passing through the "Grave-yard Perilous."

The altar was the Royal Star Regulus.

The Sun Worshippers' Grave-yard Lay On the Ecliptic Circle

Whilst quarrying stones by this Brook near Charlton Adam, Romano-British graves were found containing coins and pottery of the time of Constantinus; they are made of slabs set on edge to form a triangular cover as in Malta: among the remains were flat circular stones about a foot or more in diameter, at least eighteen were dug up as well as lion's claws, a sure sign that the graves belonged to sun worshippers; but the bones of the "first folk" mentioned in Branch 15 were not found, for the quarry was soon abandoned and is now partly built over. Sandpit Lane close by might lead to Bronze Age "folk."

A few of the finds were sent to Yeovil museum in 1928, and a record kept at Taunton Castle.

Leo's Solar Phases

Turning now to Branch 10. Title 11, it will be noticed that when Sir Lancelot passed the entrance to King Fisherman's Castle he saw two lions, one of which is the White Lion of night and winter, the lion of March that 'comes in like a lion and goes out like a lamb' in April. Sir Lancelot's is the Red Lion, the symbol of the sun in August.

Robert Brown says in The Lion and the Unicorn, that the two lions are two solar phases, diurnal and nocturnal, "and as there is but one solar orb, so he is the lion of the double lions. In the funeral ritual the Osirian or soul seeking divine union and communion with the sun god, prays:

26

'Let me not be surpassed by the Lion god; Oh, the Lion of the Sun, who lifts his arm in the hill and exclaims: I am the Lions, I am the sun.' "

W. Olcott tells us in **Sun Lore of All Ages**: "The Egyptians, Hindus, Chaldeans, Persians and Celts all regarded the lion as a solar symbol." After King Pelles' death Sir Perceval encountered the Lion.

Branch 32. Title 7.

"Perceval goeth toward the Deep Forest, that is full broad and long and evil seeming, and when he was entered in, he had scarce ridden a space when he espied the lion that lay in the midst of a launde under a tree and was waiting for his master, that was gone afar into the forest, and the lion well knew that just there was the way whereby knights had to pass, and therefore had abided there. The damsel draweth her back for fear, and Perceval goeth toward the lion that had espied him already, and came toward him, eyes on fire and jaws yawning wide Perceval aimeth his spear and thinketh to smite him in his open mouth, but the lion swerved aside and he caught him in the fore-leg and so dealt him a great wound, but the lion seizeth the horse with his claws on the croup, and rendeth the skin and the flesh above the tail."

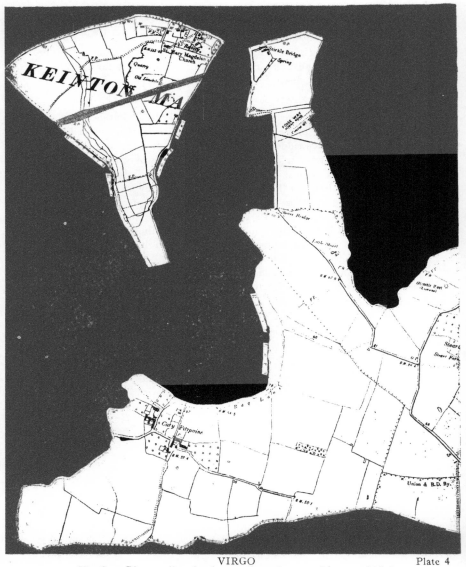

VIRGO   Plate 4
The Cary River outlines her bonnet, face, sleeve, and breast which is
marked by Wimble Toot, meaning Augur's teat.
The 'Kern Baby' is inset at the corresponding angle. The Hyperborean priestesses
"In the celebrating of the mysteries, held handfuls of corn."

28

CHAPTER II

THE EARTH SIGN, VIRGO
SHE HOLDS 'AN EAR OF CORN BY A FALL OF WATER'

SEPTEMBER and OCTOBER

Gates On the Sun's Path

Bab Cary may be the Virgin's Gate on the Fosse Way. As gates play an important part in traditions of the Temple, three land gates, and three water gates, that lie within a radius of three and a half miles from the centre at Butleigh, are here suggested.

The early British road along the hills of Mendip, that crosses the Fosse Way at Beacon Hill, sends a branch road to West Pennard, there to enter the earth sign Capricornus; this constellation was called 'The Gate of the Gods.'

Westwards, the third land entrance would have been by the Polden Hills, on the road along Walton Hill to Taurus.

The Scorpion water gate on the river Brue was called Lydford, it was the gate of death next to the gate of life in Virgo.

The second water gate lower down the Brue was the most famous, it was by Pomparles Bridge at the entrance to King Fisherman's Castle, in Pisces.

The third was on the Cary river called Somerton Gate.

But perhaps the original entrance to the Kingdom of Logres was by the River Parrett, where the effigy of the great Dog guards the junction with the old course of the Cary. Large ships could navigate the entire outline of the under part of this 'shining hound,' swept along on the flood of the tidal bore. "Messire Gawain seeth the entrance of the gateway foul and horrible like as it had been hell." **High History.** Branch 2. Title 3.

Bab is the Arab's word for gate, and it is remarkable that this original place name by the Fosse Way should remain, close to where Virgo's hand, holding out her bouquet of corn, breaks the typical straightness of that highway; this divergence exactly marks the centre of the month of

29

September in correspondence with the degrees on the modern planisphere.

Her 'Kern-Baby'

On Plate 4 we see that the profile of Virgo is outlined by the Cary river; she stands where there was once a Priory, on Wheathill, a name suggesting that what she holds in her hand is Wheat.

Still in parts of England the last ears of corn at harvest are dressed up and called Kern-Baby, or Bride or Bridget baby, which no doubt,— in the completely pagan **High History,**—was the Child that the Lady gave into the hands of the hermit when "King Arthur made much marvel, that the holy hermit washed not his hands when he had received the offering. Right sore did King Arthur marvel him thereof, but little right would he have had to marvel had he known the reason." Branch 1. Title 6.

This is the Chapel the Queen sent Arthur to, which was in "a combe of the forest," the 'Kern-baby' is partly surrounded by Combe Lane at Keinton.

Light is thrown on the subject by the dedication of the present church built in this effigy Wheatsheaf; it belongs to Mary Magdalen, and the site of Mary Magdalen's Chapel at Glastonbury once belonged to St. Bridget, the fields in Beckery close by are still called Bride's.

St. Mary Magdalen's Church at Keinton Mandeville stands in its own field, but the railway embankment and stone quarries have destroyed other fields so that the sheaf is now hardly recognizable, it is outlined by Withybed, Common, and Combe Lanes.

Having chanced upon the church in the heart of September what should we find but sheaves of golden wheat, rows of rosy-cheeked apples, and lovely flowers peeping from 'Old Man's Beard' clematis, covering the nakedness of the building from floor to ceiling: for the Harvest Festival has no doubt been celebrated here in Virgo's Wheatsheaf for nearly five thousand years.

Her stars lie around it like scattered corn, if pricked through from the planisphere on to the map; but Spica, her first magnitude star, falls in the front of her skirt, with two stars close to the Ecliptic.

30

The Cary River

The village of Castle Cary, meaning the Castle of the Castle, stands towards Camelot, under Castle Hill, where the Cary rises in five springs, one of them significantly is called Our Lady.

The river outlines the folds of her flowing robe till it reaches her breast which is suggested by a Tumulus named Wimble Toot, toot meaning teat, and wimple meaning an auger, according to the **Imperial Dictionary**. (This Toot is a Scheduled Ancient Monument.)

Near it at Stert there was a chapel, of which nothing now remains except a shed in front of the farm house; there are a few marks in the field approaching it.

Having drawn Virgo's sleeve, the river follows Rag Lane, up her throat and under her chin, round her now sunken gums, to Cary Fitzpaine, where prosperous looking farm buildings still fill her mouth with plenty: in **Doomsday Book** this place was called Cari.

Then, outlining the nose, it passes under a bridge to give her a high bonnet.

The river now crosess the Fosse Way to the hind leg of the Lion, to outline the under part of his body.

"The Paled Bar"

When King Arthur first rides to this Castlecaryland—as it was called in the fourteenth century—he "sees at the entrance a spear set bar-wise, and looketh to the right"—which implies he is turning sunwise—"or ever he should enter therein, and seeth a damsel sitting under a great leafy tree." Another translation is "he seeth at the entrance a paled bar." Branch 1. Title 6. In Heraldry a 'bar' is horizontal and a 'pale' is vertical.

S

The Damsel is the Virgin as she was before her many metamorphoses: she is sitting under the Tree of Life, and warns him of Leo thus: "the land and the forest about is so perilous that no knight returneth thence, but he is dead or wounded."

Nevertheless, King Arthur crosses the bar to cut off the head of a black giant, with whose blood the Damsel heals the wound in his arm,

31

for it is the head of Draco; whose stars fall along the arm of this Somerset Hercules.

No sooner do we turn off the Fosse Way—towards Charlton Adam— skirting the hand of Virgo, than we come to Stickle Bridge, which marks the turning up one side of her Wheatsheaf; this is Withybed Lane, a blind lane, so continuing along Broadway we reach The Barton, written in large print on the O.S. Map; it is said to mean barley enclosure, in Old English. But here was also that "Bar" which the Damsel under the tree mentions: did the fifteen stones edging the field called Stones (shown on a former O.S. Sheet 63 S.E.) mark it?

No record has been kept of their origin though on Glebe Land; they look now like mile stones.

On the other side of the railway arch from Stones is an Abbey (Farm) with Church and Cross. There was once a Priory not far away; but despite these tantalizing names the village of Charlton Adam is only a very faint echo from a forgotten past, for those "folk of religion" are as dead as Adam.

"The Sepulchre"

Branch 32.   Title 11.

"The lady made make a chapel right rich about the sepulchre that lay between the forest and Camelot, and had it adorned of rich vestments, and established a chaplain that should sing mass there every day. Sithence then hath the place been so builded up as that there is an abbey there and folk of religion, and many bear witness that there it is still, right fair."

According to the above quotation, the chapel was "between the forest and Camelot," and Perceval's sister built it, for she was the Damsel Virgo, as the **High History** says earlier in the same Title she "should be Queen." She tells King Arthur all about her brother when Arthur re-crosses "the bar" after witnessing the dismemberment of the Black Knight.   Branch 1. Titles 8 and 9.

Now the reason for trying to locate this "sepulchre" is, that "one of them that helped to un-nail Our Lord from the Cross" was buried there, see Branch 15. Titles 23 and 24; and as the stars of the constellation Crater fall on the Abbey fields, at Charlton Adam, on the same Solstitial

32

line as Stones before mentioned, it appears that Crater i.e. the Cup, was the "sepulchre" at the foot of the Sun Cross at that time, which gives us the explanation why it would only open to Sir Perceval who won the Grail.

Melkin the Bard sang:

"Amid these Joseph in marble,
Of Arimathea by name,
Hath found perpetual sleep:
And he lies on a two-forked line
Next the south corner of an oratory
Fashioned of wattles*
For the adoring of a mighty Virgin
By the aforesaid sphere-betokened
Dwellers in that place, thirteen in all."

Translated by the late Dean of Wells.

Should the above astronomical interpretation be correct, the marble coffin of St. Joseph would lie here, where the Crater stars fall, for Leo's "graveyard perilous" close by (where the Ecliptic circle passes through its tail), has already been partly excavated and marked on the official maps Romano - British Cemetery.

---

* Wattle means wicker hurdle made of withies, see Withybed Lane on illustration, south-west of Virgo's 'Kern-Baby.' The stars of Crater fall due south of this.

33

CAMELOT

"Four great zones of sculpture, set betwixt
With many a mystic symbol, girt the hall:
And in the lowest beasts are slaying men,
And in the second men are slaying beasts,
And on the third are warriors, perfect men,
And on the fourth are men with growing wings,
And over all one statue in the mould
Of Arthur, made by Merlin, with a crown,
And peak'd wings pointing to the Northern Star.
And eastward fronts the statue, and the crown
And both the wings are made of gold, and flame
At sunrise till the people in far fields,
Wasted so often by the heathen hordes,
Behold it, crying, 'We have still a king.' "

Tennyson's **Holy Grail.**

In **Branch** 3. Title 5, of the **High History,** Sir Gawain "found the fairest **meadow** land in the world, and saw a castle appear nigh the forest on a **mountain,** and it was enclosed of high walls with battlements."

This prehistoric castle of Camelot which guards the Kingdom of Logres on the south east was no myth.

Mr. Burrow in his **Ancient Earthworks and Camps** of Somerset, page 74, tells us:

Cadbury Castle—associated in folk lore and legend with the mystic Camelot of Arthurian legend—adjoins the picturesque hamlet of South Cadbury, Castle Lane leads up to the north-west angle of this mighty fortress of 18 acres, girt in all three sides of its great triangle by four immensely steep banks with ditches between—42, 26 and 38 feet deep from the bottom of the ditch to the top of the bank,—which seem to have been the work of giants rather than men. And, to add to their mysterious grandeur, these trenches were not even earthwork but were carved in the solid rock.

The **Little Guide** says "the interior 'ring' is faced with wrought masonry."

Mr. Burrow tells us again: "The hills and slightly elevated places of Somerset were occupied for a considerable period by the Goidels or Celts;

34

in fact, it is considered that the great fortress of Cadbury (Camelot) may very reasonably have been the citadel from which this great western area could be best administered in a military sense. After the Goidels and Celts came the Brythons, or Britons . . . These new-comers were conversant with the use of iron, as well as bronze, and in their turn they entered into a struggle for supremacy in Somerset . . . The language they used was the Kymric form of the Celtic Language . . .

Then about 200 B.C. Britain was invaded by another Celtic tribe— the Belgae from the North of France . . . These people settled down with their predecessors, so that when Julius Cæsar with his cohorts landed in Britain, the area of Somerset seems to have been divided in a peaceful way between the Brythons, who held the Western half, and the Belgae."

It is important to remember that though Romanized, these Britons were not expelled from the "Kingdom of Logres," south of the river Axe, before 658 or 682 A.D. when the Saxons drove them to the Parrett river: but by all the conquering races this kingdom seems to have been held in respect, judging by the place names, for in so many cases the meaning, if not the actual word, has been retained.

Logres probably extended from the Severn in the north-west, for about thirty miles to the south east, and from the River Axe to the Parrett, which is roughly a distance of seven miles.

Beyond, on the surrounding hills, can be seen, outlined against the sky, the camps of early British settlers, but none of them boast the mass of legend that clings to Camelot.

Much has been written about the gold and bronze ornaments and other remains found from time to time in the immediate neighbourhood, telling of those four, or perhaps five, great waves of conquest before the Christian Era, but how little about the worship of the sky god Camulos.

Camelot's High-Altar

There is to the south of Cadbury Castle, a little 'Mount Carmel,' one third the height of the Palestine hill; it occupies a superb position for a natural altar, just in front of and one hundred feet lower than Corton Beacon Hill.

Its name is Par Rock Hill, and the deeply cut lane that crosses it is called Halter Path; these names are significant, they mean Fire Altar, for Par and Bar here in the Kingdom of Logres refer to creative fire, or light.

35

The chief recorded event in Mount Carmel's history was the struggle for supremacy between the prophets of Jehovah, and the priests of Baal. After Elijah had built an altar on the Mount, fire from heaven descended and licked up the burnt offering. Carmel was sacred to Jupiter in the fifth century B.C., and Tacitus states that the mountain itself was a god; so on both these 'Carmel' Hills sacred fire and Jupiter were invoked; for John Rhys said of the sky god Camulos (in the 1886 Hibbert Lectures speaking on 'the origin and growth of religion') "we have discovered the Jupiter of the Celts, the supreme god of the Goidels." Whilst Faber before him, made out Casmilus, Cadmilus and Camillus to be the same as 'Baal the fountain of light.'

Three Other Camels

Camel Hill, which lies to the west of Camelot, once contained two catacombs, where many skeletons were found arranged in rows, with their feet turned towards the north. Just south of the hill is a place called Wales (it is between Queen Camel and West Camel) where there is an Eye Well on the edge of the river Cam: this holy well, when not flooded by the river, formerly supplied hundreds of bottles to be sent far afield by coach, for it is a sulphuretted hydrogen spring, and the water was used till recently by the villagers for curative purposes.

Branch 22. Title 5.

"Camelot, of King Arthur's, was situate at the entrance of the kingdom of Logres, and was peopled of folk and was seated at the head of the King's land, for that he had in his governance all the lands that on that side marched with his own."

The Ghostly Fire

King Arthur with two knights is said to ride every midsummer eve along the road under the Castle that runs from Halter Path Lane through the village. They are clad in shining armour, holding 'at the salute' their swords, which are tipped with flame.

That flame might represent the Sacred Fire Light that once dwelt in the original Grail. Mon. Matter says in his account of the 'Gnosticism of Philo,' (the following is a translation) :

"According to Philon, the Supreme Being is the primitive light, the source of all other light, the Archetype of light, from which emanate the universal rays illuminating the soul. It is the soul of the world and as such, it vibrates through all its particles. It in itself fills and bounds all Being; its purity and worth fills and penetrates all. It is without beginning; it lives in the prototype of Time. Its image is the 'Logos,' a form more brilliant than fire, for fire is not pure light.

This Logos was the world of ideas, by means of which God called visible things into being. This Logos dwells in God; for it is in His intelligence that the Supreme Being conceives the ideas by which He inspires the Universe."

Possibly Logres once had the same meaning as Logos for those who venerated the mystical Light of this Kingdom.

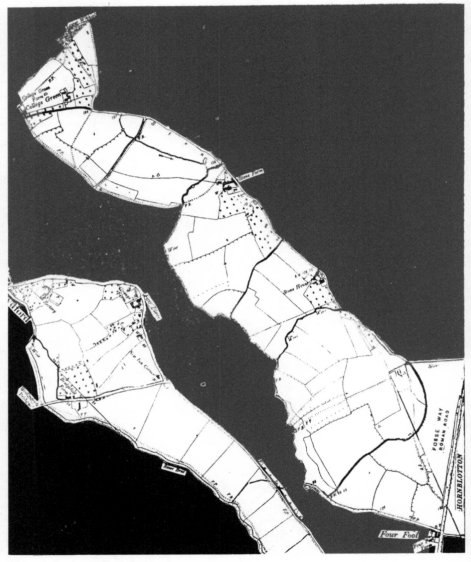

THE SCORPIONS DEATH DEALING TAIL

Plate 5

The right CLAW, inset below, actually is at right angles to the tail!
Two stars of LIBRA fall on it (there are no Scales).

38

CHAPTER III

THE WATER SIGN, SCORPIO

"HE WAS NIGH HIS END BEING AT THE POINT OF DEATH"

The High History of the Holy Graal.

NOVEMBER

Scorpio was the gigantic Warden of the Sun whom Isdubar encountered at the outset of his journey to the land of the dead; here at the entrance to the Vale of Avalon he is the guardian of the "Castle of Souls."

Originally, as in Ptolemy's list, the Scorpion was so large that it occupied the place of the later constellation Libra (the Scales) as well as that of Scorpio; this was so in Somerset, where two stars of Libra fall on the right claw.

A stone carving of the Scales is still to be seen on St. Michael's tower on Glastonbury Tor, dating from the fourteenth century, and also on Minehead Tower, where the crowned "Virgin of Light" superintends the weighing of souls.

We find in S. E. Hill's **Astrology**, page 15:

"The Virgin is often represented as holding the Balance, in connection with which fact it may be mentioned that in Manichæan tradition a Virgin of Light is met by the soul at the Gate of Heaven, i.e. at the equinoctial point in the Zodiac."

In order to draw attention to the change in the Zodiac, we suppose that the hermit, whose passing soul was being weighed, was intended for Scorpio.

Branch 1. Title 5.

"say the devils, 'But longer had he served us than he
hath served you and your Son. For forty years or more hath
he been a murderer and robber in this forest, whereas in this
hermitage (of the Scales) but five years hath he been. And
now you wish to thieve him from us.' "

"The Lady" (Virgo) answers—"I do not," and as goddess of Justice she secures the soul of the hermit Calixtus for this "Paradise," of the **High History.**

Branch 1.   Title 5.

King Arthur "would fain have sate him down before the coffin, when a voice warned him right horribly to begone thence, for it was desired to make a judgment within there, that might not be made so long as he were there. The King departed, that would willingly have remained there, and so returned back into the little house, and sate him down on a seat whereupon the hermit wont to sit. And he heareth the strife and the noise begin again within the chapel, and the ones he heareth speaking high and the others low, and he knoweth well by the voices, that the ones are angels and the others devils. And he heareth that the devils are distraining on the hermit's soul, and that judgment will presently be given in their favour, whereof make they great joy."

The Brue Flows Through the Vale of Avalon

The river Brue delineates the right claw of the Scorpion, guarding the way to Salisbury Plain; Malory says in **Morte D'Arthur:** "There was a day assigned betwixt King Arthur and Sir Mordred that they should meet upon a down beside Salisbury, and not far from the sea side."

Some have thought that Mordred was the Scorpion of death; be that as it may, the end of the Scorpion's tail can be seen very close to Arthur's horse (Sagittarius) : this death-dealing tail—where gypsies gather mistletoe before sunrise on the 12th November—is drawn between College Green and Lower Withial (White Dial) Farm, as shown on Plate 1.

Just before Arthur's "passing," we are told by Malory: "So upon Trinity Sunday at night, King Arthur dreamed a wonderful dream, and that was this: that him seemed he sat upon a chaflet in a chair, and the chair was fast to a wheel, and thereupon sat King Arthur in the richest cloth of gold that might be made; and the king thought there was under him, far from him, a hideous deep black water, and therein were all manner of serpents, and worms, and wild beasts, foul and horrible; and suddenly the king thought the wheel turned up-side-down, and he fell among the serpents, and every beast took him by a limb." It is quite clear from this dream that Malory knew all about the Zodiacal Wheel up-side-down not far from Salisbury, that the Sun fell into. It was not Stonehenge because of the beasts and serpents!

The Symbolic Human Head

In Alford Church (which is built on the head of the Scorpion) is a bench-end carving, depicting a creature taking the typical curve of a scorpion, and looking at a human head; we find the same symbol employed below a representation of the sun on the tympanum of Rollright Church, Oxfordshire, where a fish is in the act of devouring the head, symbolizing the setting or dying sun, it is surrounded by sun crosses and stars. The Knights Templars were accused of worshipping a head which was said to represent 'the Father of the Temple of universal peace,' it is very noticeable that in the **High History** the Knights and King Arthur swear by the head.

Near Alford Well Farm house there is a chalybeate Holy Well now disused.

Lyd Is Said to Mean Gate

Bridgefoot Bridge crosses the river Brue between East and West Lydford; the churches of each of these villages were built on its banks, but very little remains of the old East Lydford church; its early font was removed to the new one. The ruin is of interest, however, on account of this very proximity to the river, for the funeral 'bargiae' could moor alongside when passing through the water gate of the sacred area to go down stream to the Isle of Avalon seven miles away. Weirs to control the floods now prevent navigation. This river Brue rises near the edge of Salisbury Plain, not far from Arthur's final stand.

According to Malory's Morte D'Arthur the following were the last words of King Arthur as he lay in the funeral barge, after the battle upon "the down beside Salisbury."

"Comfort thyself, and do as well as thou mayst, for in me is no trust for to trust in; for I will unto the vale of Avilion to heal me of my grievous wound : and if thou hear never more of me, pray for my soul."

After passing over Bridgefoot Bridge on the claw of this 'Serpent-by-the-way,' the Fosse Way crosses the body of Scorpio between Four Foot (these two names seem to be a hint that we should look to our feet!) and Stone, in White Stone Hundred: it is just here that the Royal Star Antares falls.

Close by Stone is Hornblotten (Horn blow town), where there is an old bell tower detached from the restored church built of the local sun-kissed orange Oolite stone that the worshippers of golden light surely loved.

41

Leaving Stone we continue along the Fosse Way towards the Sunrise, from whence King Arthur comes to meet us: let us now mount his horse.

At a distance these Pennard Hills have the appearance of a horse and half a horse lying on its left side, hence perhaps the legend that a gate slammed in the middle of Arthur's steed: in that case Arthur's Bridge near Ditcheat would mark the tail of the half horse outside the Circle of the Zodiac.

From these hills we can look back over the low lying country of Scorpio to "many towered Camelot" ten miles distant.

CHAPTER IV

THE FIRE SIGN, SAGITTARIUS
THE HORSE

DECEMBER and JANUARY

The High History of the Holy Graal. Branch 1. Title 5.
"When the King had hung the shield at his neck and held the spear in his hand, sword-girt, on the tall destrier armed, well seemed he in the make of his body and in his bearing to be a knight of great pith and hardiment. He planteth himself so stiffly in the stirrups that he maketh the saddlebows creak again and the destrier stagger under him that was right stout and swift, and he smiteth him of his spurs, and the horse maketh answer with a great leap."

The effigy of King Arthur's "destrier" is ungainly, it must have stumbled, for its hind quarters are 350 ft. higher than its head as a result perhaps of the "stagger" and "leap."

The Pennard Hills which form its body were a bulwark of defence during invasion, and stoutly held against Cenweal the Saxon; but in 682 A.D. Centwine "drove the British to the sea." This was indeed a tragic defeat, for it meant the loss to the Celts of their Sacred Kingdom. Some think the fabled wealth was buried in it, but if there had been any the Romans would have taken it, six hundred years before: the wealth of the Kingdom of Logres consisted in the gold of the sun's rays and the jewels of the stars, for its treasure was in heaven, and locked in the secret recesses of the heart.

Despite invasion the essential outline of all the Zodiacal creatures remains intact, for they were too well designed and executed and are too huge to be destroyed, and have no value for the uninitiated; but it is noticeable that designedly, most of the feet in the composition are hidden, as in this effigy of the Horse. Orion hides his feet by sitting on them, Virgo's are well covered by her skirts, those of Capricornus wade in the mud of White Lake; but an exception has been made purposely in the case of the Bull, the Ram and the Lion.

Looking up from West Pennard station, a conspicuous 'linch' can be

43

seen on the hind leg of the Horse. Stickleball Lane outlines the whole of the front of this right hind leg from Steanbow up to Forge Well. Worthy Lane outlines the under part of the body from the stifle joint in the horse's leg towards West Pennard Church.

The upper part of the forelegs is indicated between Pilltown Farm and Newton. Church Lane marks the Horse's sternum, Breech Lane outlines its chest and then turns at right angles to draw the buttocks of Hercules. As a constellation King Arthur is Hercules.

The flourishing tail—which is a feature of the Iron Age British coins—springs from the Horse's body where the road to Hambridge branches from Drove Lane, and extends as far as the Fosse Way outlined by the stream from Hambridge (meaning bridge of the sun, which rises over East Pennard Hill) and in the tail is Huxham Green; the same meaning is thus doubly emphasized in Hu and Ham. Just north of the tail is East Pennard Church on Saxon foundations, it contains a late Norman font, representing four birds with foliated tails and large human heads; one has a goat's beard.

The road from Hambridge to Bradley Church outlines the south side of the fallen "destrier," and continues along the left thigh of the King, who, though thrown to the ground, still sits his horse's neck as close as a Centaur.

Pennard Hill Farm and Hill Farm stand 400 ft. high, on the croup of the Horse.

Almost all the stars of the heavenly constellation Sagittarius correspond with these hindquarters, Castle Lane leads to where the 'Milk Dipper' would fall. On the south side from here, fascinating little gorges run down the hill to Bradley Brook, one of them is Washing Stone Gulley, mentioned in the chapter on Leo; mistletoe overhangs it still, and foxes live in the jungle of undergrowth that spans the streams. Above the calcium carbonate encrusted stones and pools, great cultivation linches heave themselves like the ribs of this earth creature.

It is worth noticing that again we meet with both Bar and Par in Barbrook and Parbrook below the hill. Another suggestive place name is Canter's Green, by the old Court Barn on the right hip of Hercules (see illustration), as well as Breech Lane, along the under part of his breeches.

44

Though taking the place of the centaur Sagittarius, the Horse has a head; it is half hidden behind the body of the unseated King. Water courses have been utilized to outline the head and part of the bit. The watery eye is fringed by willow trees, and probably resembles all the original eyes of the effigy creatures, for these still pools reflect the sky.

Over the door of a mediæval cottage by the road side, not far from West Bradley Church, is a stone carving of an archaic looking horse; the cottage stands on the back of the neck of the Horse effigy, just where it joins the left hip of Hercules, by Westbrook House.

Sagittarius Is An Ancient Constellation Figure

The Centaur can be seen on the Norman font at Hook Norton, Oxfordshire, with other very interesting astronomical figures; also over the south doorway of Kencott Church, in the same county, where he confronts the giant head of Draco. A fine example in the round stood on the gable crest of Oakham Castle Hall, Rutlandshire, and at Worspring Priory, near Weston-super-Mare, the Centaur was found on a pavement tile.

But Sagittarius is also represented on ancient Babylonian monuments, and in India. In Egypt, Hercules stood for this constellation as he and his horse do in Somerset, and Olcott says: "The constellation is identified with the Assyrian god Assur and the Median god Ahura." Ahura is generally represented as holding in his hand a ring or crown: so in the **High History** "the Circlet of Gold" is the prize at the assembly, and King Arthur wins the crown of gold.

Branch 21. Title 25.

"The knight that had brought the crown came to the King, but knew him not a whit: 'Sir,' saith he, 'You have by your good deeds of arms won this crown of gold and this destrier, whereof ought you to make great joy, so only you have so much valour in you as that you may defend the land of the best earthly Queen that is dead, and whether the King be alive or dead none knoweth, wherefore great worship will it be to yourself and you may have prowess to maintain the land, for right broad is it and right rich and of high sovranty' "

The now practically extinct race of the Guanche in the volcanic island of Teneriffe, called their 'most high sun god' Ach-Ahura-han: it

45

used to be thought that the Guanche were the last of the Atlanteans, some think that they crossed over to Teneriffe from Spain or Morocco.

Plunket says:

"It is for the Lord Ahura, called, as here supposed, Asura, in early times, by the Ayran Manda, that I would claim the astronomical symbol of the Archer presiding over the circle of the ecliptic, or in other words, over the circle of the year, and of a year beginning at the spring equinox— a year, as has already been pointed out, distinctively Median. It is for these Ayran Manda or Medes that I would claim, at the date of 4,000 B.C., the original conception of the astronomic monogram, in which so plainly may be read an allusion to the four constellations of the Zodiac, which at that date marked the four seasons and the four cardinal points, i.e. Sagittarius and Taurus, Aquarius and Leo. This monogram was used as a standard thousands of years later by the Semitic Assyrians."

Ancient Calendars and Constellations, p. 83.

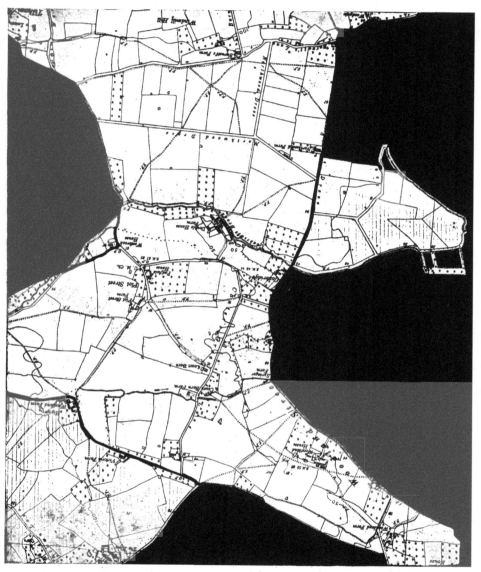

The back and "Breech" of Hercules "the King," to show that he straddles
his horse's neck, thus forming the constellation SAGITTARIUS.

Plate 6

HERCULES 'THE KING'

Like a Centaur the King sits astride the withers of the "staggering" Sagittarius horse, his back uppermost. The whole of his virile figure is drawn in outline by roads with the exception of the outstretched arm, bearded face and pointed cap, which the river Brue delineates.

Ulysses Sees Hercules in the Land of the Cimmerians
"Now I the strength of Hercules behold,
    · A towering spectre of gigantic mould,
    A shadowy form! for high in heaven's abodes
    Himself resides, a god among the gods:
    There, in the bright assemblies of the skies,
    He nectar quaffs, and Hebe crowns his joys.
    Here hovering ghosts, like fowl, his shade surround,
    And clang their pinions with terrific sound;
    Gloomy as night he stands, in act to throw
    The aerial arrow from the twanging bow.
    Around his breast a wondrous zone is roll'd,
    Where woodland monsters grin in fretted gold:"
                Pope's Translation of **Homer's Odyssey**, Book XI.

Surely Homer had the Somerset Underworld in mind!

'The Twelve Labours of Hercules' typify the passage of the sun through the Zodiacal constellations: his name conjures up centaurs, giants, apples, the Argonauts, Troy, and a funeral pyre from which he passed into the heavens.

It stands to reason that the original constellation figure of Hercules was not placed upside down, as depicted on the modern celestial globes; Homer pictured him "in act to throw" the arrows of The Archer!

Hercules was once the Saviour Melkarth of the Phœnicians, and on the Euphrates whence he came, he was known as 'The King.'

King Arthur Lies In the Form of a St. George's Cross
His commanding figure stretches across the Vale of Avalon at the head of the Sea Moors, pointing to the centre of the Zodiacal 'Wheel of Light.' Most arresting is the fact that he lies in the form of a cross, his arms parallel with the equinoctial line between Antares and Aldebaran, along which imaginary line he was made to look with his now blinded eye.

Green Hill at Tilham forms the upper portion of the bent left arm; as it is the only hill in his figure, it may have been a lookout for a 'tyler.'

The stars of the constellation Hercules exactly coincide with the effigy, and the stars of Lyra, the harp, fall on his back; a reminder of the Hyperborean's god who "plays upon the harp and dances every night, from the vernal equinox till the rising of the Pleiades," as Diodorus Siculus recounts.

The ancient Britons called Lyra "King Arthur's Harp," and they certainly knew! so it would be worth while looking up the origin of the Celtic harp. On the cross at Ullard near Kilkenny, dated 830 A.D., it is Egyptian or Assyrian in form.

Baltonsborough, pronounced Balls Borough, is in the King's beard. On the tip of his pointed cap is Catsham, for Catti was a title of British Kings, as mentioned in the chapter on Leo. The Iron Age gold coins that have been dug up in south-western England, with the letters CATTI upon them, are interesting in respect of this place name. Arthur's horse is depicted upon them with the Sun-wheel below it and the Moon above, as well as the 'three points within the circle' placed triangularly; whilst on the reverse is the Tree of Life. Ham here in Catsham means Sun, as in Hambridge, and again in Ham Street, Lottisham and Tilham, all found within the effigy of this sun god.

Godfrey Higgins quoting Bryant says: "The worship of Ham, or the Sun, as it was the most ancient so it was the most universal of any in the world. It was established in Gaul and Britain, and was the original religion of this Island which the Druids in after times adopted."

Glaston Twelve Hides

We have read in the **High History** that King Arthur "lies at the head of the Moors Adventurous:" out of these low-lying moors rises Glastonbury Tor, not four miles distant, so that the history of the famous Isle of Avalon is also the history of 'Balls Borough' to some extent. It is in the Eastern division of Glaston Twelve Hides Hundred.

The effigy outlines—like the prehistoric white horses of the Berkshire and Wiltshire hills—suggest hides: so that, whatever the derivation of the word, in all three of its meanings it helps to describe the effigies, for they resemble skins or hides laid upon the ground; they are here **hidden** or "concealed" from view on account of their great size, and "A Hide was

49

a measure of land in old English times, varying in extent, primarily the amount considered adequate for the support of one free family and its dependents, and defined as being as much land as could be tilled with one plough in a year."

Why were the Glaston Twelve Hides specially famous? William of Malmesbury says that "Twelve Hides of land" were presented by "three Pagan Kings" to the "twelve disciples of St. Philip;" but as that was nearly two thousand years ago nobody knows which were the particular hides the Pagan Kings allotted. It is strange that in some of the Mumming plays Arthur is "in the tanning trade;" "he swears he'll tan my hide." In any case King Arthur's effigy lies in Glaston Twelve Hides.

The Sun a Ball of Gold

"The Castle of the Ball" of the **High History,** appears to have been Baltonsborough; where stood the historic Norman water mill, the destruction of which the Glaston monks deplored so bitterly in the time of Bishop Jocelyn; an old house near the mill still retains the name of Gate House.

The Lord of the Castle of the Ball "that sate on a mounting-stage of marble, had two right fair daughters, and he made them play before him with a ball of gold."

Branch 6. Title 8.

A dwarf with a scourge, suggestive of one of the old gods, is also associated with this castle; Zeus and the Pharaoh both held a scourge; in India it is called the sungal.

The arm of Hercules (Arthur) crosses Wallyer's Bridge further down stream. From West Town, Coxbridge Drove draws the right side of his body, then passing Coxbridge in his waist to his thigh, Woodland Street swells over the leg muscles down to the bent right knee near Havyatt.

Our illustration, Plate 6, shows this superb line expressive of virile manhood.

The leg, after making a square bend at the knee, vanishes behind the head of Capricornus, the outline of which crosses it at right angles; its horn, Ponter's Ball, lies almost alongside the knee.

Whilst looking at this map it is important to notice the drawing of

The Flying Bull, and the other bulls on inn signs represent Taurus; whilst the Red Lion, Ram, Goat, Fish and Ring, Wheatsheaf, etc., are also easily recognizable. There are innumerable Dragons, Suns, Moons and Stars, and the Green Man stands for one of the Nature Giants which are the subject of these notes. Heraldry abounds with such star symbols.

CHAPTER V

THE EARTH SIGN, CAPRICORNUS
"THE KING OF CASTLE MORTAL"

JANUARY

The High History of the Holy Graal. Branch II. Title 2.

" 'But I tell you of a very truth, the King of Castle
Mortal is the most fell and cruel that liveth, wherefore ought
none to love him for the felony that is in him, for he hath
begun to war upon King Fisherman my uncle, and chal-
lengeth him his castle, and would fain have the Lance and
the Graal.' "

Capricornus is identical with Pan, of whom it has been said, 'Pan's
horns represented the rays of the Sun, and the brightness of the Heavens
was expressed by the vivacity of his complexion.'

The splendid line of the neck, shoulders, and back of the effigy, is
drawn by the road which runs from Ponter's Ball past West Pennard to
Steanbow; but the most important feature of the beast is its horn,
Ponter's Ball; in this earthwork, which is five-eigths of a mile long and
twenty-one feet high, Bronze Age and Early Iron Age remains have been
excavated. (See Ponter's Ball on my original 1929 map. Plate 7.)

It was the Castle of Inquest to which Messire Gawain went, thinking
to get round that way to King Fisherman's Castle, as he had been turned
away from the other entrance near Street, so Gawain learns Pan's version
of the strange things he has seen.

Branch 6. Title II.

" 'Sir, many things have I seen whereof I am sore
abashed, nor know I what castle this may be.' 'Sir,' saith
the priest, 'This castle is the Castle of Inquest, for nought
you shall ask whereof it shall not tell you the meaning.' "

The horn of Capricornus was the 'horn of plenty,' Cornucopia. Olcott tells us "the emblem of the Cornucopia is a masonic emblem, and
corroborates the fact that the major part of masonic symbols has an astronomical significance."

56

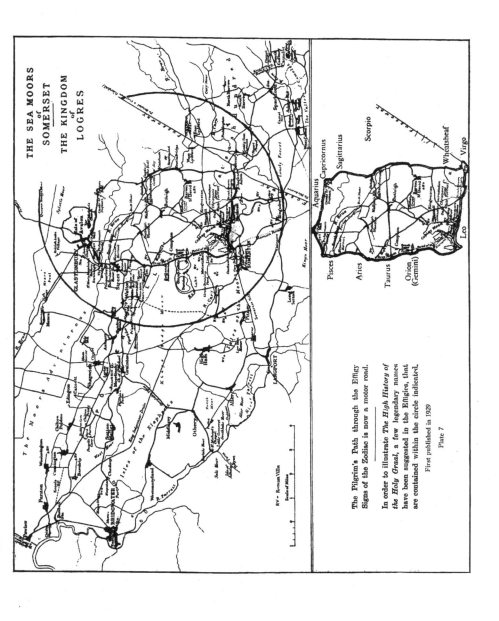

THE SEA MOORS
of
SOMERSET
and
THE KINGDOM
of
LOGRES

The Pilgrim's Path through the Effigy
Signs of the Zodiac is now a motor road.

In order to illustrate *The High History of
the Holy Graal*, a few legendary names
have been suggested in the Effigies, that
are contained within the circle indicated.

First published in 1929

Plate 7

Capricornus is seen on Babylonian Boundary Stones, and was the Goat god Mendes in the Egyptian Zodiac.

Branch I Title 1.

"Of this lineage was the Good Knight for whose sake is this High History treated. Yglais was his mother's name: King Fisherman was his uncle, and the King of the Lower Folk that was named Pelles, and the King that was named of the Castle Mortal, in whom was there as much bad as there was good in the other twain, and much good was there in them."

As we see from the above Perceval the Good Knight is not without a leaven of goat; his effigy the Phœnix soars above it, for, outlined by a footpath, the nose of Capricornus is pressed against the base of the Tor at Northwood Park Farm, a picturesque building of 1480; it lies below and east of Wick, where grow the two so-called Druid's Oaks, Gog and Magog.

The Cave of the Rising?

It is thought the Knights Templars guarded the Spring that flows forth at Paradise above Wick; certainly its lovely valley might have been looked upon as the 'cave of the rising' (which, according to ancient Akkadai, belonged to Capricornus), it is surrounded by impressive 'cultivation terraces.' A passage now fallen in, under Glastonbury's Fair Field, penetrated Tor Hill from Chalice Blood Spring, and may have come out somewhere here on the same level, for the tradition was that the sun entered a tunnel in the west at sunset and came out in the morning on the other side; it has also been said that Avalon means "passage residence.' However that may be, the waters flowing down from Paradise spring, bathe the feet of Capricornus, who watches for the rising sun at 'The Gate of the Gods.'

For hundreds of years he watched the Winter Solstitial Sun halt in its downward path, and then return to gladden the earth once more; those must have been fearful hours of suspense and subsequent rapture, for the priests of Capricornus which is said to hold the 'Double Ship' in readiness for the new born Sun.

Whether the prehistoric earthwork called Fountain's Wall is meant for that solar "Galley" of this King of Castle Mortal, it would be hard to say; but its outline is not unlike a primitive 'dug-out' canoe lying on its side; there is a real one in Taunton Museum that was found deep in the peat on these Moors, and some of them date back to the Neolithic Period.

Whitelake river outlines the under part of Capricornus, it could be said to "war upon" the two hills beneath which it flowed, belonging to King Fisherman and King Pelles. Queen's Sedge Moor stretches away to the north, outside the Zodiacal Circle of effigies, and the river also "wars" upon" that watery land belonging to the "Queen of the Maidens."

Branch 18. Title 19.

> "But now behoveth you achieve another matter. All they of the land of King Fisherman your uncle have abandoned the New Law, and returned to that which God hath forbidden. But the most part do so rather perforce and for fear of the King that hath seized the land."

So Sir Perceval ejects the King of Castle Mortal from his stolen lands as well as from the Queen's Land, and the King.

> "smiteth himself right through the body, and falleth all adown the walls into the water, that was swift and deep, in such sort that Perceval saw him." Branch 18. Title 33.

The water he fell into was that of Red and Whitelake rivers below Perceval's effigy.

Joseph the Tin Merchant

North-east of Two Lake Meeting is Tinhouse Farm, a name suggestive of Phœnicians, who may have worked the lead mines in the Mendip Hills four miles away. It is known that tin was mined in Cornwall in the Bronze Age and exported by the prehistoric Atlantic route to the Mediterranean, and perhaps to Ur. A sceptre made of tin was dug up in Glastonbury Lake Village.

In Branch 21. Title 5, we read "My name is Arthur and I am of Tin Cardoil," he was said to have been born at Tintagel.

In **St. Joseph of Arimathea at Glastonbury,** the Rev. Lionel Lewis, M.A. tells us "Joseph was a tin merchant." This is interesting because Malay and Sumatra have traditions of the prophet Joseph amongst tin workers, as we have amongst ours. Here is one of their many charms quoted from W. W. Skeat's **Malay Magic:**

58

'I know your origin, O man of penance
Whose dwelling was upon the hill of Mount Ophir,
(You sprang) from a son of the Prophet Joseph
who was wrath with his mother,
Because she would eat the hearts of the birds
of Paradise.'

There are three birds in the Somerset "Paradise."

Another charm is:

'O Grandfather King Solomon, Black King Solomon,
I desire to fell these woods,
But it is not I who am in charge of these woods,
It is Yellow King Solomon who is in charge of them,
And Red King Solomon who is in charge of them.
Rise, Rise, O Ye who watch it (the tin),'

A connection is possible between the tin miners of Sumatra and Malay, and primitive lead-mining in the Mendip Hills; but however that may be, this Joseph and King Solomon tradition is inextricably bound up with the Grail legends.

Photographs taken from the air have revealed lead smelting works in Dolbury Camp near Banwell, "certainly used in the Iron Age," see **Archæology of Somerset,** by D. P. Dobson.

The caves of Mendip, which Mr. Balch excavated and describes in his books, abound with remains from the Pleistocene Age onwards, and provide plenty of evidence respecting early settlement in this neighbourhood. A Bronze Age axe-head was found at Gough's Cave in 1934, which is only one more to add to the long list of those dug up in Somerset.

KING ARTHUR'S QUEEN

Branch 26. Title 2.

" 'Listen, so please you, to me, and all these others, listen! Madeglant of Oriande sendeth me here to you, and commandeth that you yield up the Table Round to him, for sith that the Queen is dead, you have no right thereof, for he is her next of kin and he that hath the best right to have and to hold it; and, so you do not this, you he defieth as the man that disheriteth him, for he is your enemy in two manner of ways, for the Table Round that you hold by wrong, and for the New Law that you hold. But he sendeth you word by me, that so you will renounce your belief and take Queen Jandree his sister, that he will cry you quit as of the Table Round and will be of your aid everywhere.' "

As we see from the above, King Arthur obtained this Round Table of the Stars through his marriage with the **pagan** Guenievre; she must have belonged to that earlier Water worshipping stock, which element was symbolized all over the world by snakes and women, in conjunction with the Pole Star Tree of Life.

This would explain Lancelot of the Lake's passionate love for her; most of his Lion effigy, representing sun and fire, is outlined by water; and being on so large a scale, it takes the place of the water sign Cancer, as well as of Leo.

The Dendera planisphere represents Leo standing on Hydra the water snake; Lancelot's beloved Guenievre is 'The Queen of the Serpents,' for the stars of Hydra's head and shoulders fall along the whole length of his body, outlined by the river Cary.

The beautiful ivory statuette from Crete, of about B.C. 2700, now in the Art Museum of Boston, represents this 'Snake Priestess,' of whom Colonel Waddell tells us in his profusely illustrated **British Edda**, calling her Guen-ever or Eve.

In the **High History** Lancelot's love for the Queen is expressed thus:
"So dearly do I love her that I wish not even that any
will should come to me to renounce her love, for never no
treason have I done towards her, nor she towards me."

Such language is typical of the hidden elemental meaning through-ought the **History** "drawn into Romance."

It will be remembered that the Lion's head is repeated universally on fountains in Europe, Asia, Africa and America; and also on water spouts, as at Somerton where it fittingly adorns the old Market Cross; it can be seen as a gargoyle on many churches in the neighbourhood.

On the modern picture of the stars, Hercules 'the King' is seen grasping three Hydra heads: according to Greek legend the 'hydra head in the centre was immortal' and 'was buried under a rock.'

It is likely that when the Bronze Age and Early Iron Age conquerors took possession of this Iberian land, they married its women who were associated with water and the earth gods; this might partly account for the effigy Round Table, horse, and "crown of the land" belonging to their Queen Guenievre, whose coffin we are told by the High History was in the Isle of Avilion, from which flows the Blood Spring; for those who laid out this Temple of the Stars were water lovers, water was their Queen.

Even to-day on the mountain passes of Madeira can be seen the tiny stone altar, laid in a natural cavity, to honour a pendant root resembling a snake. On the centre of the altar a fir cone is placed—"a prominent religious symbol in Assyria"—and in front, fir needles are pegged together to form a triangle, whilst the whole is sprinkled with pink and yellow flowers, and three evergreen twigs stuck up behind.

Tree and Snake worship is too big a subject to follow up here, but it is worth remembering that in Arthurian literature women sitting under trees haunt the springs of water.

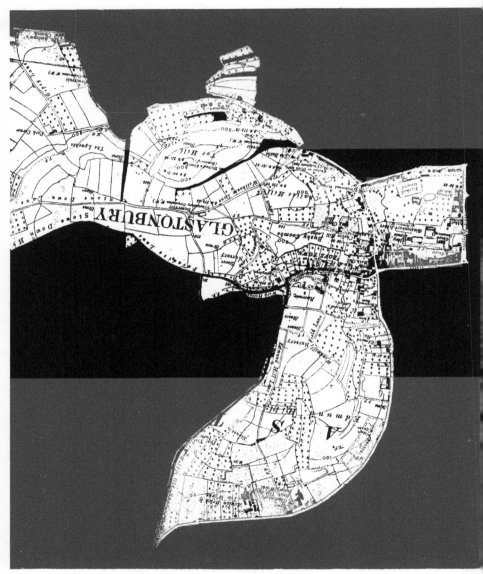

ISLE OF AVALON

Plate 8

The Effigy Phoenix flying towards the Sunrise turns its head to drink from
the Blood Spring, which is the CUP of this AQUARIUS.

CHAPTER VI

THE AIR SIGN, AQUARIUS
THE WATER BEARER

FEBRUARY

The Water Bearer effigy, of Glastonbury's Isle of Avalon, resembles a Phoenix with outstretched wings, turning its head to reach the lifegiving waters of Chalice Well Blood Spring; for the Druid's well forms the Urn of this Aquarius, and has always been associated with the Holy Grail. That being so, the astronomical point of view throws considerable light on it, for the Aquarius Cup received the rays of the sun at the Winter Solstice, and those of the moon at the Summer Solstice, about 3000 B.C.

The Universal Legend of the Cup of Immortality

Since the **High History** tells us Sir Perceval inherited the Isle of Avalon, he impersonates hereditarily this Phœnix; so the following story, taken from Donald Mackenzie's **Indian Myth and Legend,** will show him as Giant Phœnix bearing his Cup.

Once upon a time immortality (ambrosia or amrita) was robbed from the gods by Garuda, **half giant, half eagle.** This "lord of birds" was hatched from an enormous egg 500 years after it had been laid by Diti, mother of giants; his father was the Pole Star. Diti caused the amrita to be taken from a Celestial mountain, where it was surrounded by terrible flames, moved by violent winds, which leapt up to the sky. Assuming a golden body, bright as the sun, Garuda drank up many rivers and extinguished the fire. A fiercely revolving wheel, sharp-edged and brilliant, protected the amrita, but Garuda—having broken the revolving wheel—flew forth with immortality contained in the 'Moon Goblet.'

"In Teutonic mythology it is snatched by Odin from the giants of the Underworld, and is concealed in the moon." Thus Mr. Mackenzie speaks of the "persistent legend regarding the ambrosia which gave strength to the gods."

On the islands of Java and Bali, Geruda is depicted fleeing with the famous Cup, either in his hand or on his head; sometimes he carries Vishnu, who holds the revolving Solar Wheel.

63

The Round Table of the Holy Grail is a Solar Wheel

Glastonbury Tor looks down upon another such wheel, for we read in W. W. Comfort's translation of **La Queste del Saint Graal,** chapters 6 and 8: "After that table there was another like it . . . That was the Table of the Holy Graal, which gave rise to so many and great miracles in this country" (one being that it fed four thousand people). "Now, fair Sire, in the meadow which you saw there was a rack. By this rack we must understand the Round Table, for just as in the rack there are spindles which separate the compartments, so in the Round Table there are pillars which separate the seats." This exactly describes the Solar Wheel.

As one hundred and fifty bulls were feeding at this rack, it must have been no ordinary table to feed them as well as four thousand people! and we are told it was "in a meadow."

The Round Table of the Sun in Somerset measures ten miles in diameter, and consequently is well able to provide food for 150 bulls and 4,000 people.

The Aquarius Moon Goblet Described.

When Perceval captured the celestial mountain of Avalon, he came into possession of the "moon goblet" Chalice Well, famous for its strength-giving properties.

It has been said that this Druid well is a radio-active chalybeate spring; the iron in the water stains the stone over which it flows, golden red, also a rare fungus floats on the surface, resembling clots of blood. It is said that the huge stones used in its construction are of the same formation as those at Stonehenge; one single block encloses three sides of the well mouth. Miss Buckton was the owner of the Well for many years.

But neither this well, nor the Christian Chalice, was the Graal of the **High History.**

Branch 6. Title 19.

"Messire Gawain looketh at the Graal, and it seemed him that a chalice was therein, albeit none there was as at this time."

So we see that the later "chalice therein" was not the original Graal, for there was no chalice at that time.

The High History tells us "King Arthur beheld all the changes, the last whereof was the change into a chalice." Branch 22. Title 3. How can we account for this?

The Five Cups, That King Arthur Beheld

Commencing with the **fifth**, we are told Christ's blood was collected in the Chalice of the Last Supper; but before that, the Blood Spring at Glastonbury was obviously the Sun and Moon worshippers' Holy Well, for whereas the sun at the winter solstice poured its rays into this **fourth** (Aquarius) cup, the moon did so at the summer solstice.

As mentioned in the chapter on Virgo, another constellation, Crater the Cup, was receiving the sun's rays at the summer solstice, 4000 B.C. (Plunket's **Ancient Calendars and Constellations.** Plate II). Now, this ancient constellation was the "symbol of the vault of heaven," it may be called for that reason the **third** cup; and as the Temple of the Stars in Somerset represents "the vault of heaven" inverted on earth, it was probably the **second** Grail; the **first** being the starry universe.

It is on this (first) Grail that Messire Gawain looks in Branch 6. Titles 18, 19, and 20, for "he looketh up," as well as down upon the Table, where the "three drops of blood" stand for 'three points within the circle,' and the "twelve ancient knights, all balled" are the twelve constellation figures.

> "The Master of the Knights beckoneth to Messire Gawain. Messire Gawain looketh before him and seeth three drops of blood fall upon the table. He was all abashed to look at them and spake no word. . . . And the Master of the Knights summoneth him again by word of mouth, and telleth him that if he delayeth longer, never more will he recover it. Messire Gawain is silent, as he that heareth not the knight speak, and looketh upward."

Sir Perceval sees the (second) Grail mystically described in Branch 35, Titles 2 to 8.

The Effigy Phœnix

Those who have stood on Glastonbury Tor and watched the sun go down over the Severn Sea, seemingly in a conflagration, drawing after it vast wings of cloud—for cloud wings are characteristic of the Vale of Avalon—can picture the thought that inspired the architect of the effigy Phœnix; this eagle typified the sun being purified in fire at sunset, to rise again from the ashes of night; Perceval was this spiritual sun.

Messire Gawain "seeth well that albeit the night were dark, within was so great brightness of light without candles

65

that it was marvel. And it seemed him the sun shone there. Wherefore marvelled he right sore whence so great light should come."

A circle drawn around the Phœnix, one miles and three-quarters in diameter (the centre being on the breast by Paradise Lane) will be seen to touch the points of its wings and tail; this circle would enclose its traditional 'nest of **cinnamon**.'

As the body and wings were obliged to fly towards the sunrise, the head was turned backwards to reach the regenerating Blood Spring, necessitating difficult modelling, hence the remarkable linches, like spiral steps mounting up under its throat; they can be seen from a great distance.

The line along the edge of the beak is drawn by the Pilgrim's Path up the Tor, originally marked by the 'Druid stones,' a few remain though much worn. The motor road from Glastonbury to West Pennard outlines the top of the beak, for the head is lying on its side (like those of all the effigies), the crest consequently falls below this road.

The Phœnix is drawn by ancient tracks, and water. Chalice Hill forms part of the body; the sacred precincts of the Abbey lie on its tail. Two old roads to Wells outline the West wing; the terraces on South Down Hill, model the East wing; Paradise Lane indicates the breast; Norwood Park Farm stands on the outer edge of the East wing, and The Linches form the upper joint of that wing.

The road that outlines the beak turns east along Ashwell Lane, and then north, in order to outline the top of the head and the back of the neck. The great cultivation terraces called Chapels, that are approached by Coxwithy Lane, form the crest which hangs down southwards.

The Tree of Life is the Pole Star "Pillar;" the Royal Star Cross is the "Cross of Gold"

Branch 6. Title 17.

"Over against him was a pillar of copper whereon sate an eagle that held a cross of gold wherein was a piece of the true cross."

THE ROYAL STAR CROSS
combined with
THE POLE STAR TREE
or "pillar of copper" on which sat the eagle.

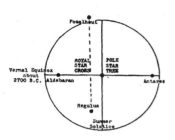

The old arms of Glastonbury Monastery were a white shield on which was placed vertically the stem of **a green tree with the branches lopped off,** a similar stem was placed at right angles to form a cross: a fitting symbol of the fate of the stellar original and Ygdrasil.

Confirmation of the idea of the eagle sitting on the pillar of copper holding the cross, is found in the accuracy displayed in laying out this Temple of the Stars: for instance, the Royal Star Fomalhaut, when transferred from the planisphere to the map, falls on Crab Tree Drove (which is on the left of the road to Wells between the tip of the West wing and Fountain Wall, near the Lake Village). A line drawn on the map between this corresponding position of Fomalhaut and that of Regulus in Leo, passes through the Bird's claw, the centre of the Royal Star Cross, and the centre of Christian's Cross, to the Lion.

The Crest of the Phoenix
This Crest or "golden comb" has the name Coxwithy, perhaps meaning cock's comb widdershins, as the bird's head is turned to reach the Blood Spring. It is made of five or more great terraces, called in **The British Edda** golden tablets.

"There maun all afterwards
Live under the same laws.
The golden tablets,
They found in the grass
These were of the olden days,
From Attar's head (eagle's head).
Unsown earth were they
Wax into till'd acres."

And again from The British Edda (Colonel Waddell's translation).

"The best spurred one of the Asas,
The golden combed
She awakes the householders
At the Aryan Father's.
But another clawed one
Is far in the earth aneath (at Eden)
The Sooty Red Hen."

The Effigies Were Purposely Designed to Be Invisible, and Now— the Key Having Been Lost—Can Be Traced Only On the Large Scale Ordnance Survey Sheets, or From the Air

It is easier to see the Phœnix' outline on the O.S. Sheets than from the top of Glaston Tor; that applies to all the Zodiacal Creatures, for they are so vast it is impossible to make out their drawings hidden in woods, under hills, or by houses, and too exhausting to follow them on foot; this explains why only initiates could see the Grail.

The curves of rivers and hills suggested living creatures to early man, but it needed a race of artists who understood how to measure the heavens as well as the earth, to resolve these existing natural forms into a circular design to fit the stars; it was 'an art founded on the principles of Geometry.' Half the outlines of seven Giant figures are drawn by natural water courses, which rather points to the idea that Mother Earth first suggested the design, though the scientific knowledge required to adapt it undoubtedly came by the same route that "Joseph the tin merchant" used from the East.

The Castle That "Never Stinted of Burning"

St. Michael's Tower crowns Glaston Tor; many churches in the neighbourhood have the same dedication, probably like this one, they stand on the site of pre-Christian fire altars.

High up on the tower is the fourteenth century stone carving of an eagle; and due south, on Wooton Hill Farm, a very fine one is represented, again with head reverted and wings fanning as in the effigy Phœnix; it is said to be the Evangelistic Eagle.

The Tor commands a fine view of the greater part of the area occupied by the effigy constellations, and on a fine day, of South Wales across the Severn Sea: on the skyline can be seen some of the prehistoric camps and beacons of the Mendip, Quantock, Wiltshire and Dorsetshire hills which surround and formerly protected the Sacred Area below. This Druids' Tor must be the castle described in Branch 35. Title 15, of the **High History,** because it belonged to King Pelles before Sir Perceval took it.

The Phœnix Castle and Twelve Chapels

"He seeth the hermit at the door of the chapel, and asketh him what the castle is that hath caught fire thus. 'Sir,' saith the hermit, 'I will tell you. Joseus, the son of King Pelles, slew his mother there. Never sithence hath the castle stinted of burning, and I tell you that of this castle and one other will be kindled the fire that shall burn up the world and put it to an end.' Perceval marvelleth much, and knew well that it was the castle of King Hermit his uncle. He departeth thence in great haste, and passeth three kingdoms and saileth by the wastes and deserts on one side and the other of the sea, for the ship ran somewhat a-nigh the land. He looketh and seeth on an island twelve hermits sitting on the sea-shore. The sea was calm and untroubled, and he made cast the anchor so as to keep the ship steady. Then he saluteth the hermits, and they all bow down to him in answer. He asketh them where have they their repair, and they tell him that they have not far away twelve chapels and twelve houses that surround a grave-yard wherein lie twelve dead knights that we keep watch over."

The twelve knights, coffins, altars, hermits, chapels, and houses refer to the twelve zodiacal constellations.

The Effigy Creatures

Now let us take a bird's eye view from the Tor, as did the architect in chief of this Nature Temple.

We can picture, though we can no longer see, the Zodiacal creatures spread out below like a great circus; for the travelling circus of today, in its round tent with central pole supporting it, is a survival from prehistoric times.

The Lion is out of sight from the Tor, for he is lying on the slope of the hills opposite Somerton, in order to get the full glare of the south sun in his months of July and August.

Towards the East, Virgo reclines, outlined by the Cary river; she

69

looks like an old witch with a broomstick, dressed in high bonnet, and flowing garment sufficiently voluminous to hide the host of babies she has produced from its folds.

Further East, with the right claws lying along the river Brue, sprawls the gigantic Scorpion, waiting to catch the unwary.

Then next in the ring comes Hercules like a Centaur, for he has been thrown on to the shoulders of his kneeling horse, south west of the Pennard Hills.

North of this horse of the sun, the Goat lies, showing off his wonderful horn, Ponter's Ball.

These Zodiacal effigies would be on the designer's left hand as he stood on the head of the Phœnix "eagle" looking south. Here again **The British Edda** gives us a verse:

> "The (Sun) Eagle flies o'er it
> There Fialla (the Falcon)
> Hunts for fishes."

For the fishes are Pisces, on the architect's right hand side.

Fisher's Hill leads up to one of them, which may have been the famous 'Severn Salmon,' the 'Salmon of Knowledge' that 'fed on red hazel nuts' floating down to its mouth on the Blood Stream, through Read Mead.

And there below, stretching past Plunging nearly to Wallyer's Bridge, floats the Whale, outlined by the river Brue.

Next to the second fish lies the bound Ram of Walton and Street, its feet higher than its body: it should have a Golden Fleece of corn.

Along that same Polden ridge can be seen the top of the Bull's neck, the Hood Monument stands on its ear.

Beyond these hills appears the Giant Orion of Dundon Beacon, which almost completes the magic circle.

At the Pole, is the head of the fire breathing Dragon, and there are two Dogs in the troop, one inside and one outside the Ring, besides a "Griffin" bird, a Dove, and "the Ship of King Solomon."

This vast picture was in truth a dial, laid out for the sun and moon to ride round.

The Archetypal Microcosm

The 'Glaston Abbey' clock has been in use in Wells Cathedral since 1392. Above its dial knights tilt against one another every hour, showing that the clockmaker connected Knights in shining armour with the idea of Time; the motto on the dial is: 'This round ball denotes the archetypal microcosm,' a better translation 'This sphere denotes the universe its archetype.' Surely it is intended as a reminder of the ten mile wide dial of its native place, which has the real sun and moon revolving round it. The clock depicts them in their appointed circles, the outer one is divided into twenty-four parts reminiscent of the Round Table of King Arthur at Winchester, with twelve light and twelve dark divisions radiating from the centre. An important feature is that the clock shows the moon in all its phases, and on the four outer corners, four angels hold the sun's **giant heads**, which play so mysterious a part throughout the **High History**.

Sir Perceval's Uncle Called Him Par-Lui-Fet

The uncles from whom Sir Perceval inherited or won this Isle of Avalon were—King Fisherman, i.e. Pisces.; King Pelles, i.e. Aquarius; and King of Castle Mortal, i.e. Capricornus; they correspond with dark and wintry months, for Perceval ruled over the first quarter of the year, as well as the night.

The Hermit in the following quotation is King Pelles, whose name for Perceval Par-lui-fet" he hath made him of himself" also means fire made him. In Branch 5. Title 4, he has just laid aside his shield with the sun upon it, implying that the sun has set.

" 'If he should rise, as sick as he is, none might prevent him nor hold him back, but presently he should arm him and mount on his horse and joust at you or any other; and so he were here, well might we be the worse thereof. And therefore do I keep him so close and quiet within yonder, for that I would not have him see you nor none other, for and he were so soon to die, sore loss would it be to the world.' 'Sir,' saith Messire Gawain, 'what name hath he? 'Sir,' saith he, 'He hath made him of himself, therefore do I call him Par-lui-fet, of dearness and love.' 'Sir,' saith Messire Gawain, 'May it not be in any wise that I may see him? 'Sir,' saith the hermit, 'I have told you plainly that nowise may it not be. No strange man shall not see him within yonder until such time as he be whole and of good cheer.' "

71

A Land of Fire and Sun Worship, Kindred to That of Egypt

It must have been an inspiring sight when Glastonbury Tor stood in the midst of hundreds of Beacon Fires tossing their flames up to the night sky from the surrounding hills, a survival of the Beltane Fires of May Day. In living memory at least a hundred were still lighted on great occasions, and blazing tar barrels annually rolled down the streets of Bridgwater till a few years ago.

Below the crest of the Phœnix lie the fields called Actis: Lower Actis is the tract of land opposite to Plunging. Now the **Classical Dictionary** says: "Actis, Son of Sol, went from Greece into Egypt where he taught Astrology, and founded Heliopolis."

And Diodorus Siculus. **Historical Library**, Book 5, Section 57:

"The Sons of Helios (or Sol) were distinguished from other men by their education and their knowledge of Astrology. They made many discoveries useful to navigation and rules concerning the seasons. Tenages, who had more natural talent, was killed by his brethren out of jealousy. The crime having been discovered all the culprits took to flight. Macar went to Lesbos; Kandalanus to Cos; Actis landed in Egypt and founded the city of Heliopolis."

And who was Sol, the father of Actis? Lempriere's dictionary says again:—

"Sol (the sun) was an object of veneration among the ancients. It was particularly worshipped among the Persians, under the name of Mithras, and was the Baal or Bel of the Chaldeans, the Osiris of the Egyptians, the Adonis of the Syrians. Apollo, Phœbus and Sol are universally supposed to be the same deity."

As Cinnamon Lane lies next to Higher Actis, let us see what the Encyclopedia says about Cinnamon:

"Cinnamon has been known from remote antiquity, and it was so highly prized among ancient nations that it was regarded as a present fit for monarchs and other great potentates. It is mentioned in Exodus." The Phœnix is represented in the Peterboro' Bestiary inside its ball of spices looking at the sun which will set it on fire; again, another bird is there illustrated on its nest of cinnamon in the top of a tree.

Did Actis of Heliopolis Leave His Name Below the Tor? or Is the Land Named After Him? If so, Why, and By Whom?

The Nile, by Wallace Budge, gives us the following concerning this Prince of Heliopolis; it is translated from a papyrus in the British Museum:

A Hymn to Ra when he rises in the Eastern Sky.
"Homage to thee, O thou who art Ra when thou risest
and Tmu when thou settest. Thou risest, thou risest; thou
shinest, thou shinest, O thou who are crowned king of the
gods. Thou art the lord of heaven, thou art the lord of
earth, thou art the creator of those who dwell in the heights,
and of those who dwell in the depths. Thou art the ONE
god who came into being in the beginning of time ... O thou
mighty youth, thou everlasting sun, **self-begotten, who didst
give birth to thyself;** O thou mighty One of myriad forms
and aspects, King of the world, Prince of Heliopolis, lord of
eternity, and ruler of everlastingness, the company of the
gods rejoice when thou risest, and when thou sailest across
the sky."

In Egypt a soul "might make its transformation into the Phœnix
which flew to Heliopolis."

As already pointed out in this chapter, Sir Perceval is said to have
"made him of himself," and to have a sun on his shield, so **he** must have
been the Glastonbury Actis, this **self-begotten** Prince of Heliopolis,
transformed into a Phœnix.

Glastonbury Abbey's Pyramids, and Her Prehistoric Lake Villages

We have stood on the Tor to witness the last flaming moments of the
setting sun, and its ethereal rising after a night of starry splendour, and
have seen Perceval's uncles, the constellations, dance their dance around
the Pole Star; now let us descend by the Pilgrim Path and go to the
Abbey grounds where a few feet from St. Joseph's Chapel stood those
tell-tale Pyramids that were said to mark Arthur's grave! One was 28
feet high and the other 26 feet high, as William of Malmesbury saw them.

Almost opposite the Golden Wheel Tea Rooms which display the
Signs of the Zodiac as a signboard, is the Museum; it contains a little
of what has been laboriously recovered from the two British Lake Villages lying in the Moors below Glastonbury. Arthur Bulleid in his **Lake
Villages of Somerset** tells us about objects of Flint, Amber, Glass, Jet,
Pottery, Tin, Lead, Bronze, Iron and much else, including the hearths in
the round huts (these hearths are ornamented with circles), which he
discovered and dates "provisionally" at B.C. 250 to 300.

Of the skulls dug up here, Bulleid quotes Sir William Boyd Dawkins as saying that all of them belong to the oval-headed Mesaticephalic section of the inhabitants of Britain, and :

"They are physically identical with the small dark inhabitants of the Basque Provinces of France and Spain . . . The same race occurs in Italy, in Greece, the Greek Islands and in Asia Minor, and in Northern Africa, being represented in the West by the Berbers, and in the East, as Prof. Elliot Smith has shown, by the primitive Egyptians and their descendants among the fellaheen."

The Meare Lake Village collection is exhibited in the County Museum at Taunton Castle and also a number of relics from the Godney Lake Village.

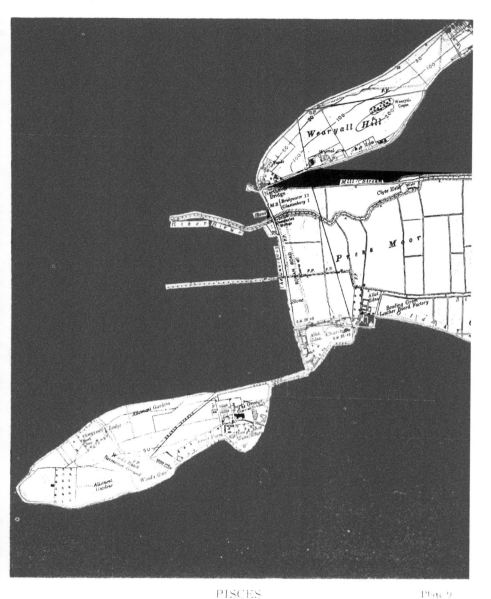

PISCES   Plate 9

The Line connecting the Fishes passes over the Perilous Three bridges on the
tail of the Whale, between Street and Glaston's Isle of Avalon.
Though not shown here, the Whale's tail extends over Hulk Moor.   75

CHAPTER VII

THE WATER SIGN, PISCES and CETUS

MARCH

From the Air View we see that Glastonbury's Wearyall Hill forms one of the Fishes; the other is in Street: the Whale extends from Hulk Moor west of Pomparles Bridge almost to Wallyer's Bridge, along the river Brue.

The High History of the Holy Graal. Branch 10. Title 9.

"So far hath he ridden that he is come forth of the forest and findeth a right fair meadow-land all loaded with flowers, and a river ran in the midst thereof that was right fair and broad, and there was forest on the one side and the other, and the meadow lands were wide and far betwixt the river and the forest."

" 'Lords,' saith Lancelot, 'is there no castle nigh at hand nor no harbour?' 'Yea, Sir,' say they, 'Beyond that mountain, right fair and rich, and this river runneth thither all round about it.' 'Lords, whose castle is it?' 'Sir,' say they, 'It is King Fisherman's.' "

From King Fisherman's Castle—which is the Wearyall Hill Fish effigy—one looks down towards the north west on the prehistoric Lake Villages of Godney and Meare; it was doubtless their idol, for a fish was supposed to swallow the sun as it sank down into the sea, thus explaining King Fisherman's sickness and death.

The idea of a fish god was originally brought by the Early Phœnicians from the Euphrates; many books have been written about him under his different aspects of Ea, Poseidon, etc., and at Lydney Park on the Severn he was represented in a pointed cap hooking a salmon, for the Celtic fisher god Nodon 'god of the abyss' had a sanctuary there.

Branch 10. Title 9.

"There was a knight within in the midst of the boat that was fishing with an angle, the rod whereof seemeth of gold, and right great fish he took."

76

Babylonian seal-cylinders, and coins found at Gades in Spain bear this symbol.

A carving in Manor House Farm at West Down, near Ilfracombe, shows him as Orpheus playing on his lute, with a long fish's body and tail and fins, and the four points of the compass marked by four lions' heads around him; the date of the carving is 1560. Above it is the winged horse of the Templars, whilst in another room there can be seen a remarkable plaster relief of an elaborate subject realistically treated, and dated 1624.

This relief bears on our subject, the Temple of Time. Winged Father Time on crutches is riding in a chariot drawn by two white harts(the car of the Kingdom of Logres had three white harts), the wheel of the vehicle is encircled by numbers up to twelve as on a clock dial, the spokes of the wheel being formed by the St. George's and St. Andrew's crosses. Behind the white harts is a Norman Church; to the right a huge sun shines over the heads of Adam and Eve in the garden of Eden, indicated by a tree and flowers below. Eve is in an enclosure on wheels which Adam guides. At either side of the relief two giant women support flowers and fruit on their heads, one holds the earth and the other an anchor, thus representing earth and water as women do in the **High History.**

Walking along the front of the composition are four bearded men, the first pointing either to the number 6 on the clock wheel or to the earth, the fourth points to the sun; two younger figures in line with them point to Adam and Eve in the garden.

In **The Shepherd of Hermas** we read of these "six young men" and also of the Virgins who "stood mannishly as if about to carry the whole heaven."

The damsel who accompanied the car of Logres drawn by three white harts, spent some of her time at the Fish hill, for she was the River Brue which flows through the Kingdom typified by the car: King Arthur remarked "such Kingdom as is this of Logres," when he had "sent without to see the costliness and fashion of the car."

Branch 2. Title 1.

"There is without this hall a car that three white harts have drawn hither, and lightly may you send to see how rich it is. I tell you that the traces are of silk and the axletrees of gold, and the timber of the car is ebony. The car is covered above with a black samite, and below is a cross of gold

77

the whole length, and under the coverlid of the car are the heads of an hundred and fifty knights whereof some be sealed in gold, other some in silver and the third in lead. King Fisherman sendeth you word that this loss hath befallen of him that demandeth not unto whom one serveth of the Graal. Sir, the damsel that beareth the shield holdeth in her hand the head of a Queen that is sealed in lead and crowned with copper, and I tell you that by the Queen whose head you here behold was the King betrayed whose head I bear, and the three manner of knights whose heads are within the car."

We have already seen in Chapter IV that the river Brue outlines the head of "the King" Hercules, and in Chapter V that the head of "the Queen" (Hydra) is outlineed by the Cary river; so this again points to Adam and Eve in the garden of Eden, for we are told this King was betrayed by this Queen. The above quotation is illuminating in other ways; it mentions the "cross of gold the whole length," that the eagle held (Chapter VI.).

The idea of the Damsel's Car is very ancient; at the Ashmolean Museum, Oxford, can be seen the early iron age Votive Cauldron from Kein Glein, held by a tall female figure above her head; she stands in the centre of a four wheeled Car on a sun wheel, surrounded by tiny knights and two stags. It is interesting to compare the Lucera bronze tripod in a case close by, for all these symbols are found in our Arthurian legends, including the bull.

The Sun Beamed On All Sides Although the Night Was Dark

"King Fisherman's Castle" approached by Fisher's Hill, was called Weary-all because the thousands of pilgrims who went to Glastonbury had reached their journey's end here, like the setting sun. When Lancelot saw the sun King, he must have been swallowed by the Fish already, for "the night was dark."

Branch 10. Title II.

"The Knights lead him before King Fisherman in a chamber where he lay right richly. He findeth the King, that lieth on a bed so rich and so fair apparelled as never was seen a better . . . such a brightness of light was there in the chamber as that it seemeth the sun were beaming on all

78

sides, and albeit the night was dark, no candles, so far as Lancelot might espy, were lighted therewithin."

But before Lancelot, Messire Gawain had been to King Fisherman's Castle.

Branch 6. Title 17.

"They lead him into the chamber where lay King Fisherman, and it seemed as it were all strown and sprinkled of balm, and it was all strown with green herbs and reeds ... and under his head was a pillow all smelling sweet of balm, and at the four corners of the pillow were four stones that gave out a right great brightness of light."

Saith King Fisherman:

"And greater cheer would I make you than I do were I able to help myself, but I am fallen into languishment."

The ancient pilgrim ways outlining the Fish are now used as motor roads and the drawing has been perfectly preserved by them, but below the Fish's belly on the south side of the hill two fins can be distinguished from the air view, also the faint outline of the gills comes out on the photo.

The Line That Ties the Two Fishes on to the Whale

The second Fish lying in Street, contains the modern cemetery. Abbey Grange occupies the place in its tail where one star from Pisces fell, another star is marked by Street Churchyard which is circular and consequently ancient, and a third star lay on Press Moor, in the Whale's tail.

The following is Messire Gawain's experience of the Three Bridges (which form the line that ties the two Fishes on to the Whale).

Branch 6. Title 15.

"Much marvelled he that he found the bridge so wide that had seemed him so narrow. And when he had passed beyond, the bridge, that was a drawbridge, lifted itself by engine behind him, for the water below ran too swiftly for other bridge to be made. The knight draweth himself back beyond the great bridge and Messire Gawain cometh nigh to pass it, and this seemed him as long as the other. And he seeth the water below, that was not less swift nor less deep, and, so far as he could judge, the bridge was of ice, feeble

79

and thin, and of a great height above the water, and he looked at it with much marvelling, yet natheless not for that would he any the more hold back from passing on toward the entrance. He goeth forward and commendeth himself to God, and cometh in the midst thereof and seeth that the bridge was the fairest and richest and strongest he had ever beheld, and the abutments thereof were all full of images. When he was beyond the bridge, it lifted itself up behind him as the other had done, and he looketh before him and seeth not the knight, and is come to the third bridge and nought was he adread for anything he might see. And it was not less rich than the other, and had columns of marble all around about, and upon each a knop so rich that it seemed to be of gold."

One of the Bridges was called 'Pons Periculosus' in 1415, which recalls the fable repeated by Leland, that King Arthur cast his sword into the river here, where the sun sinks down in the glories of the sunset; but nothing could look more prosaic than it does adapted to modern requirements, despite, its being still called Pomparles.

The Brue is divided into three streams above this Bridge. When repairs were being made to "the third Bridge," just by the Fish's mouth, huge piers of golden Ham Hill stone, which still support it, were uncovered, but they are now hidden under a mass of concrete; perhaps they are Roman, since Roman pottery was found under the ancient road running parallel with the present one, and also above on Wearyall Hill; but flint implements have also been found there.

So here, connecting Street with Glastonbury, were the "Three Bridges" crossing the three streams, that the Knights who followed the Quest were obliged to pass over on their way to The Royal Isle; when they were adorned with images, and their marble columns had "golden knops," they must have formed a beautiful watergate through which the sacred barges passed to the Holy of Holies at the centre of the circle of effigies.

The Castle of the Whale

Branch 35. Titles 11 to 15, tells about Gohas of the Castle of the Whale, who "had a ring at his feet and a collar on his neck with a chain whereof the other end was fixed by a staple into a great ledge on the rock."

The road joining the Fishes to the Whale passes over his tail, and as all modern pictures of the star constellations join the Fishes on to the Whale by a ring and a chain, it is clear that the **High History** refers to the same tradition.

On Javanese Zodiac cups a whale takes the place of the Fishes.

The **High History** says "this great land is his own that is so plenteous," for he is entirely outlined by the river Brüe and Old Rhyne.

Branch 35. Title 10.

"in all these islands of the sea is there none that hath any puissance but he only, and so assured is he that no dread hath he of any. For none that is in this land durst offend against him."

Near Baltonsborough, Wallyer's Bridge is an important place-name, for it either means Waellas (Celts), or Whale's bridge; it is here that the arm of Hercules crosses the River Brue.

Since both Hercules and the Whale indicate the direction to take, we will now explore the centre of the circle of Cosmic Deities, returning to the circumference later.

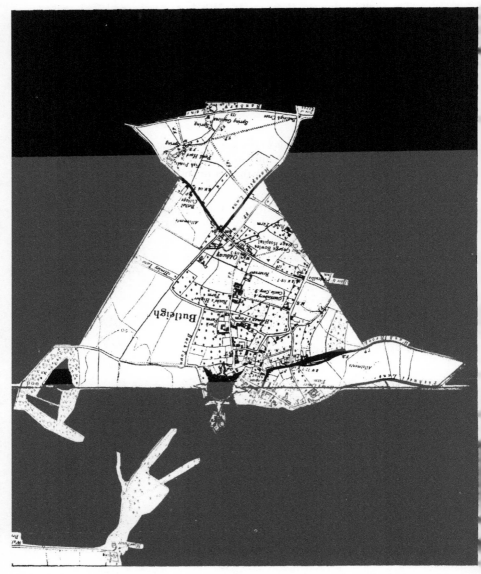

Three Points in the Centre of the great Effigy Circle are suggested by: A Serpent's Head on a "Crown" (Park Wood), A Finger (Wash Brook), and the enclosure dominated by Butleigh Cross. The base of the triangle thus described, indicates the Equinox B.C. 2700 if the line is projected west through the eye, and "bell" which marks the Royal Star Aldebaran in the effigy Taurus (to which the great Finger points), and east to the place of the Royal Star Antares in the body of the effigy Scorpio.

In order to show that the alignment of the Nature Temple is not exactly due east and west the points of the Compass are given at the centre of the base line.
Plate 46

THE ANCIENT POLE STAR IN URSA MINOR IS HERE MARKED BY A SERPENT'S HEAD ON A "CROWN" WHICH WAS THE POLE OF THIS TEMPLE OF THE STARS

The High History says :

"The serpent seeth him, and cometh toward him, jaws yawning, and casteth forth fire and flame in great plenty. Perceval thrusteth his sword right through the gullet."

The equinoctial line of 2700 B.C. passed through the "gullet" of this serpent as shown on the illustration, plate 10.

It is remarkable that the North Somerset Mummer's Play should have kept alive the tradition of the "Black Prince of Paradise, born in a fiery hole" (see **Mummers' Plays**, by R. J. Tiddy), for he can be none other than Draco, whose "giant head" guards the fiery hole of this Pole Star. The hole corresponds astronomically with that mysterious 'Enclosure-of-Life,' formed by four stars of Ursa Minor once called 'the little Fiery Chariot,' and held by Arabs and Mohammedans to be 'the hole in which the earth's axis found its bearings.' Kochab, meaning 'The Star,' was the Lord of this 'abode of the essence and spirit of life' or 'place of the crown of the land,' for it was of 'supreme importance as the Pole Star when Taurus led the year' as R. Brown says in **Primitive Constellations**. In that case it superseded *a* Draconis the previous pole star.

As for that 'crown of the land,' the **High History** tells us that the Crown and the Round Table belonged to Queen Guenievre who, if she be the same as Eve, would feel quite at home with the serpent Draco, and the Pole Star Tree of Life, and we noticed that on the old plaster relief of the Wheel of Time at West Down, Eve is in an enclosure on wheels which Adam is pushing, possibly it represented this 'little Fiery Chariot' (Ursa Minor). (For 'her crown and land' see Branch 21. Titles 24 and 25.)

The crown that is universally known as having a snake's head on it, is the crown of Egypt, and it is singular that the unusual shape of Park Wood at Butleigh, where we find the serpent's head, is not unlike the White Crown of Egypt in outline. Branch 35. Title 5, tells us that the crown was suspended over the Masters' table and the hole ! so we must conclude that the "crown of gold" covered Draco's "hole."

"And while he was thus looking, he seeth a chain of gold come down above him loaded with precious stones, and in

83

the midst thereof was a crown of gold. The chain descended a great length and held on to nought save to the will of Our Lord only. As soon as the Masters saw it descending they opened a great wide pit that was in the midst of the hall, so that one could see the hole all openly."

It is in Park Wood that we can trace, by means of wide grass paths amongst the trees, the perfect drawing of a snake's head, "jaws yawning" towards the west; on the map it looks as if it were protruding from a choker collar; this is probably intended for its hole.

The snake's head, or "dragon's head," fittingly described as "giant" in the **History,** measures about 880 feet, there are no earthworks to distinguish it, or the supposed "hole;" nevertheless it exactly corresponds with the centre of this Circle of effigies.

Judging by the hundreds of birds that flock from the surrounding neighbourhood to roost in the branches of the trees in this "crown," one would almost imagine that the snake had some queer fascination for them; but as a matter of fact, Park Wood is carefully preserved and fenced in with barbed wire and a ditch; let us hope it will be kept a bird sanctuary for all time.

The High History of the Holy Graal is written about what it calls "the Earthly Paradise" and "Eden," so it is worth turning up the **Encyclopædia Britannica** (11th edition) and reading "Paradise," for the interesting information there given.

Branch 35. Title 12.

"he seeth in a little islet a knight that is mounted up in a tall tree that was right broad with many boughs. There was a damsel with him, that had climbed up also for dread of a serpent, great and evil-favoured, that had issued from a hole in a mountain. The damsel seeth Perceval's ship coming, and crieth out to him. 'Ha, Sir,' saith she, 'Come to help this King that is up above, and me that am a damsel!' 'Whereof are you afeard, damsel?' saith Perceval. 'Of a great serpent, Sir,' saith she, 'that hath made us climb up."

Of Draco we read in **Star Lore of All Ages:**

"This serpent is the guardian of the stars (the golden apples) which hang from the Pole Tree in the Garden of Darkness, or Garden in the West, the Garden of Hesperides."

Saith the Welsh Bard:

"The proper place of this delicate tree, is within a shelter of great renown."

"Incorruptible is the tree which grows in the spot, set apart (the sanctuary) under its wide envelope."

"The sweet apple tree is like the Bardic mount of assembly; the dogs of the wood will protect the circle of its roots." (Canis Major and Canis Minor being the dogs.) See **Mythology and Rites of the British Druids**, by E. Davies.

A-wassailing the apple tree, is a Druid custom annually kept up in Somerset. Making a ring round the largest tree in the orchard this verse is sung:

> "Old apple tree, Old apple tree,
> We've come to wassail thee
> To bear and bow apples enow
> Hats full, caps full, three bushel bags full,
> Barn floors full, and a little heap under the stars."

A bucket full of cider is put under the trees, and bread that has been toasted is dipped in it, and stuck in a fork of the branches for the birds.

'The Wisdom of the Serpent' must refer to the knowledge which Draco possesses of the Nutation of the earth's axis, and Precession of the Equinoxes, or the change by which the equinoxes occur earlier in each successive sidereal year. The contemplation of seven successive pole stars was bewilderingly upsetting to the calculations of astronomers; no wonder Draco became the "Devil!" but the 'Seven Glorious Ones' have had many more good names than bad, for pole stars never set.

It was into the hole of the Pole that Horus drove the serpent monster, thenceforth called Ba, which perhaps gives us the origin of that word in the Kingdom of Logres, for Ba was its fire soul; it is not only Perceval who destroys one of its fiery heads, for Arthur (Hercules) cuts off another, as we have already observed.

In Branch 18. Titles 6 and 7.

Perceval "dealeth him a great blow on the shield in such sort that he cleaveth it right to the midst thereof where the dragon's head was, and the flame leapeth forth so burning hot on his sword that it waxed red-hot like as was the Knight's sword."

85

"The dragon's head turneth it toward his lord in great wrath, and scorcheth him and burneth him to dust, and thereafter departeth up into the sky like lightning."

The Illustrated London News of July 22nd, 1933, contained a reproduction from an Akkadian Cylinder seal of the seven headed fire-dragon that 'Hercules' killed 2500 B.C.! The expression used by Dr. Henry Frankfort in describing this discovery was: "astonishing in its implications." Its seven heads would be the seven pole stars.

At the commencement of **The High History of the Holy Graal,** King Arthur's squire dreams that he stole a golden candlestick belonging to the brother of a black giant. The taper that he removed from the candlestick may have been a pole star, for it burned "in the midst of the launde" with three others, around the body of the "knight that lay dead in the midst of the chapel," i.e. the three stars of Ursa Minor with Kochab.

Branch 1. Title 3.

"This squirè marvelled much how this body was left there so lonely, insomuch that none were about him save only the images."

THE GREAT FINGER OF THE EQUINOX
Marks the Second Point of the Suggested Triangle; It Lies South West
of Butleigh Church, Compton Street by Rocke's Lower
Farm Outlines It

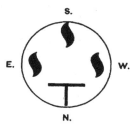

"THREE DROPS OF BLOOD" ON THE GRAIL TABLE
The Symbol means Jehovah

Branch 6. Title 19.

"Messire Gawain looketh before him and seeth three
drops of blood fall upon the table. He was all abashed to
look at them and spake no word."

The first Point or "drop," towards the east, has just been described;
presumably the second Point or "drop of blood," towards the west, was
the centre of the Cosmic Cross formed by connecting the four Royal
Stars of the four quarters of the sky.

We have already seen that the finger of the hand of Hercules at
Moorhouse, points toward Butleigh, but another finger, on a much
larger scale points west, into the eye of Taurus. Confirmation of this
indication is found in the name Compton Street underlying this Finger,
for the eye of Taurus lies at Compton.

The great Finger, with nail and bend of joint clearly defined, has no
earthworks; it consists of ordinary flattish fields, and is quite out of
proportion to any of the other figures; but because of the coincidence of
its position in the centre of the Royal Star Cross over head, and consequently resting on the equinoctial line of B.C. 2700, as well as marking
the second point of the triangle suggested by "the three drops of blood"
on the Table, one is inclined to believe it is part of the original Temple
design.

The name of the stream that is made to outline its south side is suggestive of ritualistic washing, it is called Wash Brook. Former Ordnance Survey maps showed the old footpath bifurcating where the jewel of a ring on the Finger might lie, near lower Rocke's Farm.

The spring that feeds Wash Brook is at Beggar's Grave—outside the Finger—where are the ruins of a circular building, with a paved floor, like a Columbarium; this stands at the lower end of a prehistoric earthwork called New Ditch, so it is probably on an older foundation.

Since we are dealing with the second point of a triangle, we cannot avoid mentioning the so-called Vesica piscis. As Sydney T. Klein says in his interesting paper on the subject, to be found in **Ars Quatuor Coronatorum**, the whole science of Geometry is based on the intersection of two circles, and the equilateral triangle is itself generated by it.

In order to form the two intersecting circles, this second point or "drop" is essential. Having formed the Vesica piscis, it gives us the third "drop" which fell upon the Graal Table, that is, the Apex of the Triangle.

It is no wonder that the triangle was called the Logos, or "World of Ideas,' for it is the basis of Geometry and Astronomy, and the triad of Religion.

The Geometrical figure of the Vesica piscis is used on seals, in architecture, miniatures, stained glass, frescoes, illuminations, tapestry, and by the Old Masters in their religious pictures to frame Our Lord in Glory.

The seventh century binding in Mr. Pierpont Morgan's collection, chosen as an illustration to Sydney Klein's article, is very interesting in this respect.

Possibly this triangle in Somerset was worked out as a test (to find the effigy Giants) by a different, perhaps Egyptian race, whose expression "the Finger of God," is significant in this respect.

That the pole of the Ecliptic, here on the fore arm of Hercules, (which is the centre of the stars of the Zodiacal Circle) was not known to them, is apparent: and they were not sure of the exact Centre of the Temple area either, which is Park Wood, Butleigh.

The same people may have added Argo-Navis under the Giant Orion, as King Solomon's ship, with the Griffon bird standing on the rudder, because the masts of that sun ship converge on the apex of this triangle.

If three more triangles are superimposed on this one as foundation, their points will indicate the position of the twelve effigy Signs around the circle.

But the original designers of this chart of the heavens, almost miracously knew the place of the Pole of the Ecliptic (how could the Zodiacal stars fall within their correct effigies when transferred from the planisphere, if it were not so?), but they did not make that their Centre; they made the Pole star Kochab the Centre of their composition. Just as on Philips' star chart our present Pole Star occupies the middle place.

THE ENCLOSURE OF THE SUN
The Apex of the Triangle

The unique idol vases from the fourth City of Troy, dated by Dr. Schliemann about 1500 B.C., show the **Three Points** on the sun bird's vase. (See pages 521, 522, 523 and 575 of **Ilios,** published by John Murray.) We shall now describe the third Point, or "drop of blood" towards the south, but still in Butleigh.

Amongst the effigies which comprise the Chart of the Stars in Somerset is one representing Argo Navis; the masts of this ship of King Solomon exactly converge—when projected on the large scale map—upon what we take to be the enclosure of the Sun, or the apex of the suggested triangle.

The convergence of the masts suggests /|\ which is the symbol of God's name.

The first volume of **Bardas,** page 17, explains the Symbol of the primitive Bards of the Isle of Britain which was "the symbol of God's Name from the beginning:" /|\

"In three columns; and in the rays of light the vocalization—for one were the hearing and the seeing." These rays penetrate Mother Earth, and she in turn brings forth her harvest of 'eternal festival;' consequently it is interesting to note that the same symbol, the Broad Arrow—pregnant with archaic religious significance—is still used as the Royal mark on British Government Stores of every description.

If the whole lay-out of the sacred area had not been planned with geometrical exactitude, we might have hesitated to believe that the convergence of the masts of the Ship on this point was intentional, and it is a coincidence that the cottage nearest to the spot where the lines meet, should be called Bethel as seen on the 6 inches to 1 mile Sheet, for it means in early Phœnician 'The House of the Supreme God.'

The space thus indicated is surrounded by the Lanes called Wood or Wooton, Harepits and Banbury, all of which names are ancient and suggestive; Ban being the name of the aborigines of Britain according to L. A. Waddell.

The western angle of this enclosure is marked by Butleigh's ancient Cross. The Romano-British road called High Street, coming from Leo, passes close by, where the old name 'Rose and Portcullis' (Inn) is a reminder of the Rose at the centre of King Arthur's Round Table at Winchester, and of another in the middle of the Glastonbury clock, as well as the expression which once meant so much, **'sub rosa;'** in the East on a certain day in the year 'the rose has a heart of gold.'

Butleigh Cross has been restored as a war memorial, and since the ground on which it stands slopes down towards the east, one looks over the valley "where lies King Arthur," to the sunrise.

Within the enclosure are two excellent springs called on the map Spring Gardens and Pond Head; they supply fish ponds of recent date that are beautiful with primroses in April; here can be seen lumps of that fantastic stone that has been formed by the mingling of these waters with sun-lit air.

The roof of Wells Cathedral Chapter House is said to have been built from this so-called tufa, brought from the Polden Hills; one wonders if it was used on account of its lightness or its sacred origin. In less than twenty years a block the size of a man is formed, and has to be removed in order not to choke up the fairy's well.

A wide strip of sandy soil runs parallel with the fish ponds, the water from which flows on past Park Buildings near Park Wood, to Shuttle Orchard on the river Brue.

Branch 2. Title 1.

> "This river was right fair and plenteous. Josephus witnesseth us that it came from the Earthly Paradise and compassed the castle around."

In the following quotation from Branch 6. Title 2, the gold and silver and ivory vessels probably represented the enclosures of the Sun, Moon and Pole Star, repeated by the triad of ghostly damsels, two of whom subsequently vanished and only one remained.

> "Therewith, behold, three damsels that come of right great beauty, and they had white garments and their heads were covered with white cloths and they carried, one, bread in a little golden vessel, and the other wine in a little ivory vessel, and the third flesh in one of silver. And they come to the vessel of gold that hung against the pillar and set therein

91

that which they have brought, and afterward they make the sign of the cross over the pillar and come back again. But on their going back, it seemed to Messire Gawain that only one was there."

"The pillar" must be the Pole Tree in the centre of this Temple layout, hence "the sign of the cross over the pillar," meaning the Solstice and the Equinox. The head of the "great serpent" marks it.

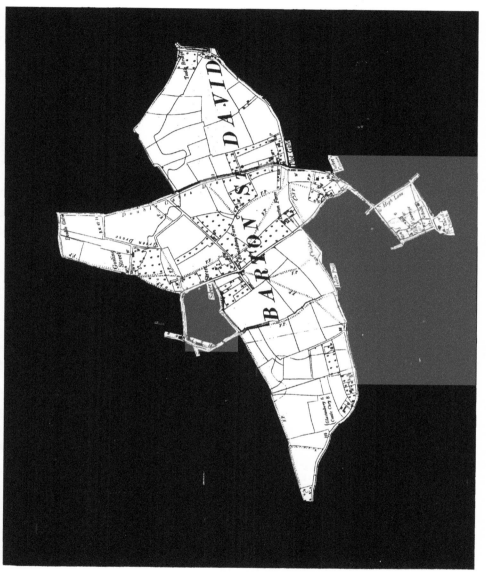

"The DOVE" that carries "The Host" is 'Parzival' (the stars of   Plate 11
'The great Plough' fall on the left wing).
Perhaps it is the third air sign in place of Libra.

93

THE DOVE

'I will address myself to my sovereign, the King of the
Air, O, Sovereign of the power of the Air.'
Quoted from Meilyr, a Bard of the twelfth century.

Around Barton, St. David lies the outline of a bird, its left wing corresponding with the stars of Ursa Major; but as it is not far from Lydford
where the right claw of Scorpio takes the place of Libra, it may have
stood for the third Air sign; if so it belonged to Perceval.

It is smaller than his two other effigy birds and, unlike them, lies
on its back; it was the Dove that carried the 'Host' in 'the Parzival.'

The road from Butleigh to Barton passes along the upper edge of
the left wing, and from the old house called Barton Farm to Lower
Barton Farm, a road outlines the under part of the bird's body, and
another road delineates its half closed right wing leading to Tootle
Bridge on the Brue. The rest of the drawing is traceable only by foot-
paths, one called Double Gate Drove leads to Double Gates on its tail.
Tootle is said to mean 'look out'; unfortunately there is very little left to
look out for on the ground, but the stars that correspond with the outstretched wing, being the important stars in the handle of the 'Great
Plough,' (Ursa Major) it is to the sky that we must look. Its eye was at
Tucker's Corner.

In **Star Lore of all Ages,** Mr. Olcott says:
"The Northern sky is in reality a great clock dial over which hands
wrought of stars trace their way unceasingly. Moreover it is a time piece
that is absolutely accurate." The Great Plough appears to revolve round
the heavens once in twenty-four hours, though it is the earth that is really
turning. He gives us in the same chapter the other names of this constellation.

In Ireland it was 'King Arthur's Chariot,' and the Druids so named
it. The French called it the 'Great Chariot,' and 'David's Chariot,' which
is interesting, for the effigy bird appears to hold the Old Vicarage at
Barton St. David, with the church and Cross of St. David in its beak.

In the Middle Ages, in different countries, Ursa Major was known as
the 'Chariot of Elias,' 'Thor's waggon,' 'Waggon of Odin,' 'Car of Osiris,'
'the abode of the Seven Sages who entered the Ark with Minos,' the
'Waggon of Our Saviour,' and 'The Brood Hen.'

To sum up, the constellation of the Great Bear or Plough was held to be the fiery Brood Hen, and appears to have carried Osiris, Minos, David, Elias, King Arthur, Thor, Odin, and Our Saviour endlessly round the starry heavens every twenty-four hours.

The Welsh Bard sings:

"I have presided in a toilsome chair, over the circle of Sidin—the circle of the Zodiac—whilst that is continually revolving between three elements; is it not a wonder to the world that men are not enlightened." See page 296, **Mythology and Rites of the British Druids.**

It is "a wonder that men are not enlightened" considering that it has always been known that the Priests of the Mysteries imitated the motions of the celestial bodies, and that they took the names of the constellations and dressed to represent the Zodiacal creatures. The theology they taught was purely astronomical.

Cynddelw, the Bard, sings of the mystic dance of the Druids:

"Rapidly moving in the course of the sky, in circles, in uneven numbers, Druids and Bards unite, in celebrating the leader."

Ursa Major contains the oldest star symbol, i.e. the fiery wheel or cross called the Swastika; it might be suggested in the circumstances that the name of the county of Somerset once had the same meaning, which is familiar to us in 'turning a Somersault or Somerset,' for the **High History,** Branch 6. Title II, says: "the car that the damsel leadeth after her signifieth the wheel of fortune;" this sign is represented on early British coins, and is a "symbol of the goddess of the silver wheel who guarded the limits of the British temple."

Besides the wheel on these coins 'the point within the circle' is shown, and also the trefoil or triad, with the horse of the Sun.

95

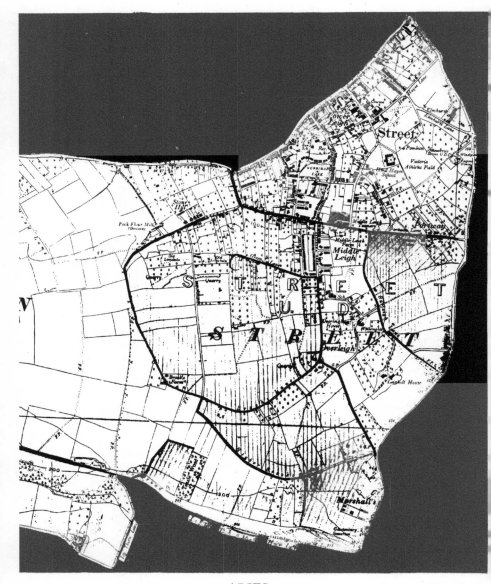

ARIES   Plate 12

Showing the reverted head and fore-foot of the traditional
Lamb and Ram.

96

CHAPTER VIII

THE FIRE SIGN, ARIES
REPRESENTED AS A LAMB, WITH HEAD AND FORE FOOT REVERTED

Aries Was Once Called the Prince of the Zodiac; the Ancient Persians
Named Him Bara; Bactria Was the Old Land of the
Zarathustra Fire Worshippers

APRIL

The **High History** says: "He had a rich clasp at his neck wherein
were many rich stones," for the stars Hamal, Sheratan and Mesartim fall
on the neck of the effigy.

Branch 6. Title I.

"Messire Gawain rode until he came to a forest, and
seeth a land right fair and rich in a great enclosure of wall,
and round the land and country-side within, the wall
stretched right far away. Thitherward he cometh and seeth
but one entrance thereinto, and he seeth the fairest land that
ever he beheld and the best garnished and the fairest
orchards. The country was not more than four leagues
Welsh in length, and in the midst thereof was a tower on a
high rock."

Aries is so small a constellation that its stars when transferred to
the map from the planisphere are found to fall around Portway; doubtless this is the explanation of the **History's** "one entrance thereinto," for
Portway has no other meaning locally (see plate 12).

On Walton Hill can be seen the remains of earthworks, perhaps
part of "a great enclosure of walls four leagues Welsh in length;" those
walls of Wal-ton are mentioned three times, and belonged to the Waellas
or Celts, for we are told the "King of Wales was lord of the land:" that
is why the Welsh Bards knew so much about this sacred Kingdom.
(Walton, and the corn mill, are marked on Map of the Sea Moors,
plate 7.)

"The tower on the high rock" probably stood where the round Norman Corn Mill (rebuilt by John Tulley in 1192, but now converted into

97

a dwelling) commands a fine view of the plain of King's Sedge Moor, and also of the Vale of Avalon; it stands on Walton Hill which forms the hind leg of Aries. The hoof is well drawn by Ivy Thorn Lane, and from the farm the road under the hill continues the outline of the foot. A large flint scraper was picked up opposite this farm: it is in Bridgwater Museum with a few other Sedge Moor implements of flint.

At Ashcott, the Walton Hill road joins the main Street road, this so called Roman road outlines the back and mask of the effigy as far as The Cross (printed in large type, on a former O.S. Sheet), near Street Church; this important name for the cross roads in connection with the Lamb, lay by the tip of the ear.

From here the road returns at right angles towards Leigh, thus outlining the back of the averted head; then passing by Portway Lane, which is the line under the jaw, it goes on to draw the joint of the reverted fore foot at Marshall's Elm; on Ivy Thorn Hill it is indicated by a deep trench cut in the rock.

This traditionally bent back fore foot extends as far as three upright stones marking the entrance to the footpath which outlines the hoof; several other stones have been broken off in the same place, and there are the remains of a flagged path leading to them from the motor road, almost opposite the turning down to Ivy Thorn Farm, two-thirds of a mile from Marshall's Elm. Continuing along the hill road we reach the Corn Mill tower again, having completed the circuit of the young Ram's contour.

From Walton Hill the outline of the bottom of the Phantom Ship, Argo Navis, is visible crossing King's Sedge Moor along Walton Drove, and in high relief the back and right side of the reclining Giant Orion can be seen (see plate 16; and plate 1 for the ship in the West).

Sir Lancelot was taken by mistake for Aries because he also represents fire; on New Year's Day he is told he "should be crowned in the fire;" that would have been about B.C. 2540, determined by the stars of the month's heliacal risings.

Branch 10. Title 4.

"Thereupon behold you the provosts and the lords of the city, and they come over against Lancelot. 'Sir,' say they, 'All this joy is made along of you, and all these instru-

98

ments of music are moved to joy and sound of gladness for your coming.' 'But wherefore for me?' saith Lancelot. 'That shall you know well betimes' say they. 'This city began to burn and to melt in one of the houses from the very same hour that our king was dead, nor might the fire be quenched, nor never will be quenched until such time as we have a king that shall be lord of the city and of the honour thereunto belonging, and on New Year's Day behoveth him to be crowned in the midst of the fire, and then shall the fire be quenched, for otherwise may it never be put out nor extinguished. Wherefore have we come to meet you to give you the royalty, for we have been told that you are a good knight.' 'Lords,' saith Lancelot, 'Of such a kingdom have I no need, and God defend me from it.' "

Presumably Sir Lancelot met the revellers on the Ashcott Road at the ancient foundation of Piper's Inn, for the **History** states, "there was much noise of bagpipes and flutes;" they may have taken him to Reggis Stone near by; three times it is mentioned that Lancelot rode by the 'plain' which is King's Sedge Moor. But Messire Gawain, to whom the castle belonged, was the proper sacrifice in this sign as we read in the following:

Branch 33. Title 4.

"if that Messire Gawain were in fear, little marvel was it, for he thought that his end had come. Meliot espied him bound to an iron staple with cords about the body on all sides so that he might not move."

Confirmation of the Effigy Constellations

On the Zodiacal relief at Stoke-sub-Hamdon Church, Leo, Sagittarius and Aries stand under the Tree of Life that has three birds in its branches. On this ancient stone carving Aries is shown holding the Cross, Sagittarius wears the pointed fire cap and is shooting an arrow at the Lion which has "pricked ears" and tongue lolling out and two of the birds are large in proportion to the Tree, whilst the third is smaller: all these peculiarities we find in our Temple of the Stars.

This early confirmation in stone is to be seen on the tympanum over the entrance to the Church; Stoke-sub-Hamdon is near Montacute and both places lie under Hamdon Hill, famous for its miles of earthworks and other prehistoric remains. The stone relief is illustrated in **High-**

ways and Bye-ways of Somerset, accompanied by the following bit of history.

On Montacute's St. Michael's Hill, the Leodgaresburg Cross of Flint was found in the days of King Cnut; twelve red oxen and twelve white cows drew it to Waltham. (Probably the local Walton is meant, because left to themselves it is impossible that the beasts would have wandered right across England, they were so close to Walton in the Kingdom of Logres "which had a cross of gold the whole length.")

However, before the battle of Hastings the Flint Rood bowed to Harold, hence the English battle cry, Holy Cross! Holy Cross! (so it certainly was no ordinary cross) and as a result of its discovery on St. Michael's Hill a college of priests was established at Montacute "in honour of the invention of the Holy Cross." Another thing to be remarked is that the cross was "glistening black" and had a duplicate beneath it of wood. It lay six miles to the south of the effigy Leo; Leo, as just pointed out, is depicted on the church close by.

In the following, Lancelot, the impersonation of the Lion, lies down with the Lamb "as it were on a Cross," and "takes three blades of grass," a significant sign in this connection as some will recognize.

Branch 20. Title 13.

> "He taketh three blades of grass and so eateth thereof in token of the holy communion, then signeth him of the cross and blesseth him, riseth up, setteth himself on his knees and stretcheth forth his neck. The knight lifteth up the axe. Lancelot heareth the blow coming, boweth his head and the axe misseth him. He saith to him 'Sir Knight, so did not my brother that you slew; rather, he held his head and neck quite still, and so behoveth you to do!' . . . The knight forthwith flingeth down the axe . . . "

The Tidal Port of The Kingdom of Logres

In the Somerset Temple of the Stars, besides that of Aries, twelve other heads are laid out to look towards the sea and sunset; this arrangement must have been a stupendous task for the designer. An additional reason for the turn of the head of Aries may be, that it looks along the Polden Hills to Down End, and to the tidal port on the Parrett river at Dunball, where there was an early British settlement; the earthworks can be seen on a level with the railway station, by the branch road to the

CHAPTER IX

THE EARTH SIGN, TAURUS
ABOUT 2700 B.C. THE VERNAL EQUINOX LAY IN THE EYE OF THE BULL

MAY

The High History of the Holy Graal. Branch 18. Titles 11 and 12.

"He seeth the bull of copper in the midst of the castle right big and horrible, that was surrounded on all sides by folk that all did worship thereunto together round about."

"Perceval was therewithin, but none was there that spake unto him, for so intent were they upon adoring the bull that, and any had been minded to slay them what time they were yet worshipping the same, they would have allowed him so to do and would have thought that they were saved thereby; and save this had they none other believe in the world."

In **The Mythology and Rites of the British Druids** by E. Davies, we read of Oxen, that "their office, in the commemorative ceremony of the Britons, was to draw the car of the lofty one, or Hu, the Patriarch god, to whom the oxen were consecrated, in solemn procession. And if this was the meaning of the memorial, the **avanc** of mythology, which the sacred oxen drew out of the lake, and which gave rise to the ceremony, must imply the identical shrine, or vehicle, which enclosed the Diluvian Patriarch."

Gwynvardd Brecheiniog, a Bard who wrote in the former part of the twelfth century, says:

"The amiable Bangu was left behind, bearing his chain."

May we infer that Taurus was the amiable Bangu who "overstrained himself, in drawing forth the **avanc,** so that his eyes started from their sockets, and he dropped down dead, as soon as the feat was achieved." (**Mythology and Rites of the British Druids,** page 140.)

The Effigy

The Bull's head lies at Compton, where Tray's Farm occupies the

105

place of the Bull's eye, and thus gives us the exact equinoctial line of this Temple of the Stars as it was first conceived; for we have already noted that the effigy Finger marking the centre of the Royal Star Cross points to Taurus.

A few carved stones such as the remains of an Early English window, and swirling quatrefoil, on the cider-press barn at Tray's Farm, speak of former buildings of importance here, to which a flagstone path leads all the way from St. Andrew's Church at Dundon.

As one stands on the top of the Bull's neck Collard Hill, and looks down south towards Dundon Beacon, it can be seen that the road draws the outline of its lower jaw; the Manor of Ivy Thorn to the west, adorns its shoulder; ivy was sacred in ancient days on account of the resemblance of its flowers to globes of stars and the holy Thorn of Glaston is well known.

The Pleiades correspond with the remains of earthworks on the West side of the Somerton road, near the turning to the Manor. About 2300 B.C. the Moon was worshipped in the Pleiades, then marking the Vernal Equinox.

The ears of the Bull, Giant, Lion, and Dog seem to have been of primary importance to these nature effigiees, that of Taurus on Windmill Hill commands an interesting view: from here the pilgrim's path up Glastonbury Tor can be seen outlining that sacred mount against the sky. Looking south, the road below the Hood Monument (which stands in the Bull's ear) draws the curves of his nose; whilst beyond one can see into the great ear of Orion the Giant, that is outlined by the camp on Dundon Hill; under this, King's Sedge Moor stretches away towards the sea shrouded in mist. Sprays of tiny white flowers fill the Bull's ear in July, they are called Enchanter's Nightshade.

It was once held that the Bull opened the year with its horns, Hatch Hill is here pierced by them, on the equinoctial line!

An Avenue of Cedars

Continuing along the hill toward Wickham's Cross, one of the horns can be seen on the right; the tip of the earthwork that outlines it points to the gateway on the left of the road through which the Processional Way supposedly passed from Butt Moor Bridge on the Brue, to Compton Dundon.

Butt Moor Bridge was the "first bridge" that Messire Gawain had to expect after leaving the precincts of King Fisherman's castle when he "goeth his way a great pace beside a great river that runneth in the midst of the valley." Many have wondered why it should have rained so much that it almost drowned him, while the sun shone on the other side of the river; the explanation is that he was riding on the Plunging "Whale," but he is told "At the first bridge you come to will it be stayed upon you," see Branch 6. Title 22.

Not far from this bridge a very narrow road leads to a majestic avenue of cedar trees which enters Butleigh Wood; the path through the woods climbs the hill to the gate by the tip of the horn of Taurus, where it suddenly emerges on to the top of a natural amphitheatre, looking down upon the Giant Orion.

Then, a deeply worn path (now completely overgrown and not shown on the map) passed down this amphitheatre, or horse-shoe curve, formed by the Polden Hills from High Ham to Priest's Hill near Ashcott.

At the bottom of this steeply inclined path, Withy Lane leads to the Bull's nose: it is a singular coincidence that a rifle range is marked on a former O.S. Sheet 63 N.E. crossing the field to the Bull's eye.

Withy Lane divided near Law's Farm, branching off to the two Red-lands, and also to join the flagstones leading to St. Andrew's Church, that saint being chosen in place of Taurus for the 'Apostolic Zodiac' when Taurus lost favour in the eyes of the Church: it is worth noting that in the Hebrew Zodiac Taurus was Joseph.

The Bell

Branch 22. Titles 2 and 3.

"and there was one behind that carried a bell with the clapper and all at his neck. 'Ha, God,' saith King Arthur, 'What folk be these?' 'Sir,' saith Pereceval, 'I know them all save the last.'"

"Then he asked the hermit that bare the bell, whence this thing came? 'Sir,' saith he to Messire Gawain, 'I am the King for whom you slew the giant.'"

Branch 20. Title 7.

"nor was there never a day so long as King Arthur was on pilgrimage, so saith the history, but he heard the sound of one single bell every hour, whereof he was right glad."

One Redland is on the Bull's dewlap, below which lies his Bell, that was "set on the ground" (on Hurst Drove) "though at this time was there no bell neither in Great Britain nor in Lesser" as the **High History** says. The narrow strips of land between its five ditches must indicate the "clappers;" astronomically they correspond with Aldebaran.

Hurst Drove leads to Ham Lane which draws the back of Orion, Mead Run lies between these two suggestive place names. There is said to be a tunnel from Hurst Farm to St. Andrew's Church "along which the fairies used to go to church" according to the farmer's wife; another story is that the ghost of a knight in armour holding a sword, stands at the foot of the pulpit stairs. (Orion's sword?)

The Red Launde of Arthurian Romance

Redlands gives us one of the most important place name clues, for the Red Launde Tourney must have been held here, about which the **History** speaks so much.

It stands to reason that the Tourney would be held at this place which corresponds with the Royal Star Aldebaran and the Vernal Equinox, then the place of the May Day festivals.

Branch 13. Title 8.

> "This high record saith that Messire Gawain hath wandered so far that he is come into the Red Launde whereas the assembly of knights should be held. He looketh and seeth the tents pitched and the knights coming from all quarters."

We read in **Celtic Druids,** page 153, "The change of the time of the equinoctial festival from the first of May to the first of April, would of course be made at the time that the equinox had ceased to take place in Taurus or May."

Beltane, the Celtic name for May-day and its festival, represented the Druidical worship of the sun god, of which the surviving ceremony in later centuries was the lighting of bonfires known as 'Beltane fires.'

Traces of these still linger in Ireland, the Highlands of Scotland and Brittany. And again G. Higgins says (**Celtic Druids,** page 291): "After all that the reader has seen, he will not have been surprised to find the Bull amongst the gods of the Druids. By a Bull, made of brass, the

108

Cimbri, Teutones, and Ambrones, swore to observe the capitulation made with the Romans on the Adige. After their defeat, Catulus took this bull and kept it in his house, as a trophy of his victory."

Again, page 132: "The remains of the worship of the bull, or the sun in Taurus, are to be met with everywhere—all over India, Persia, Greece, Italy and Britain."

The Bull's Calf

In the **High History,** King Gurgalain impersonates Taurus; he sends Messire Gawain to kill the Giant (Orion) who has stolen this King's son—obviously in the circumstances a calf!

Messire Gawain returns with the "son," having killed the Giant of Dundon Beacon Hill.

Branch 6. Titles 6 and 7.

King Gurgalain "maketh light a great show of torches in the midst of the city, and causeth a great fire to be made, and his son be set thereon in a brazen vessel all full of water, and maketh him be cooked and sodden over this fire, and maketh the Giant's head be hanged at the gate."

"When his son was well cooked, he maketh him be cut up as small as he may, and biddeth send for all the high men of his land and giveth thereof to each so long as there was any left."

As a description of a primitive sacrificial feast, the foregoing quotation is suggestive, the mention of torches, the Giant's head, the eating of every morsel of flesh, even the word bidding as in the bidding-prayer.

The next picture we have of this Bull King who was "Lord of Albanie," is as the hermit who followed the procession after he had encountered three priests on the sea-shore by an ancient hermitage: the following reply to King Arthur's enquiry respecting the bell does sound like the confused utterance of a pagan bull.

Branch 22. Title 3.

"I made baptize me before you and all those of my kingdom, and turn to the New Law, and thereafter I went to a hermitage by the sea, far from folk, where I have been of a long space. I rose one night at matins and looked under my hermitage and saw that a ship had taken haven there. I went thither when the sea was retreated, and found within the ship three priests and their clerks, that told me their names and how they were called in baptism. All three were named Gregory, and they came from the Land of Promise, and told me that Solomon had cast three bells, one for the Saviour of the World, and one for His sweet Mother, and one for the honour of His saints, wherefore they had brought this hither by His commandment into this kingdom for that we had none here. They told me that and I should bear it into this castle, they would take all my sins upon themselves, by Our Lord's pleasure, in such sort as that I should be quit thereof."

The Reason for Not Depicting More Than the Bull's Head and Right Foot

There was no room for the body of the Bull, because the effigy Ship of King Solomon "had taken haven there;" it will be remembered that only the head and shoulders of Taurus are shown in the pictures of the star constellations.

On the Dendera Temple Planisphere the Beeve with the bell on its neck is lying down in the ship; and on the ceiling of the grand portico of this temple, Taurus carries the Sun on his neck in the cup of the crescent Moon.

Before describing the effigies of those 'Great Twins' the sun and moon, the hounds of Arthurian Romance claim our attention.

110

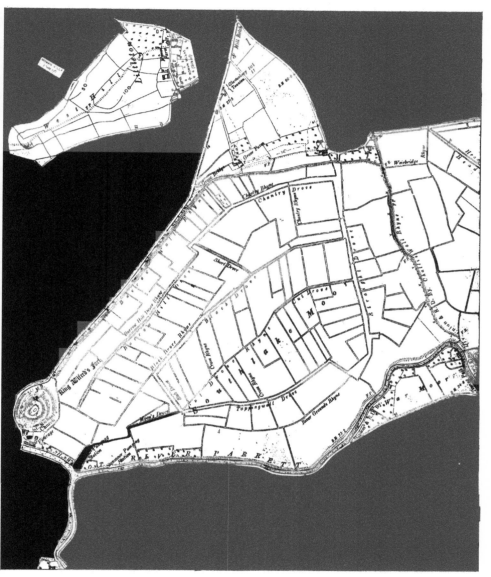

"THE QUESTING BEAST"   Plate 14
Effigy head of the great Dog near Athelney; Burrow Mount forms its nostril.
Inset is the head of CANIS MINOR.

111

CHAPTER X

THE DOGS
'THE DOG OF GWYN AB NUDD, THE BRITISH PLUTO, IS NAMED DOR-MARTH'

A great Hound guards the entrance to the "Kingdom of Logres" at Athelney; the historic fort is described as it once was, in Branch 4. Title I, of **The High History of the Holy Graal.**

"And it was compassed about of a great water, and had about it great clumps of trees so as that scarce with much pains might he espy the hall, that was right large. The river that compassed it about was water royal, for it lost not its right name nor its body as far as the sea. And Messire Gawain bethought him that it was the hold of a worshipful man, and draweth him thitherward to lodge. And as he drew anigh the bridge of the hold, he looketh and seeth a dwarf sitting on a high bench. He leapeth up: 'Messire Gawain,' saith he, . . . 'you will find my lady, the fairest and most gentle and most courteous in the realm of Logres, and as yet is she not of twenty years.' 'Fair friend,' saith Messire Gawain, 'What name hath the lord of the hold?' 'Sir, he is called of Little Gomeret.' "

It will be found when we describe **Canis Minor** that the dwarf's "lady" is the effigy Hound, which is formed by conducting channels of water between immense artificial earth-works, and by the ancient "path" bounding Aller Moor.

By means of Burrow Wall and Challis Wall, the river Cary was made to delineate the Hound's nose and collar, when that river flowed round Michels Burro into "water royal" of the Parrett; this tidal river, with a Phœnician name, outlines the under part of the Hound's jaw, throat, ribs, stomach and hind leg as far as Langport.

Between the solar names Ham Down and Huish, the tip of the tail is drawn by Wagg Drove and Wagg Lane at the place called Wagg!

Speaking of Langport it is worth mentioning the old stained glass window of Joseph of Arimathea in the church on the Hill, where he is shown holding the two cruets.

The High History says in Branch 4. Title 3, that the Lord of the hold of Little Gomeret, Marin the Jealous,

"bideth above a pool where was a spring, and maketh her enter into the water that flowed forth full cold, and gathereth saplings in the forest for rods and beginneth to smite and beat her across upon her back and her breast in such sort that the stream from the spring was all bloody therewithall."

The industry around Athelney is "gathering saplings," thousands of bundles can be seen in all stages of preparation, but chiefly standing "in the water that floweth forth full cold," stained red by the soil of Red Hill. The outline of "her back" is almost a straight line from Pathe by Allerdrove through Aller to Wearne, where the old road outlines the rump to Wearne Wyche: this was also King Alfred's "path" to Somerton.

The ear of the Hound stands up on a hill like that of the Lion, Bull and Giant, no doubt in order to listen to the "chanting spheres of prophecy." As the name of the hill is Grove Hill, the sacred grove may have been in the ear hole at Grove Farm; just south the name Chantry is retained.

North of Athelney, the district called Earlake Moor lies by the Hound's ear; not far from its mouth is Head Drove, and again another Head Drove and Head Rhyne edge Little Hook on its collar (Challis Wall). Which names prove the recognition of this effigy up to comparatively recent times.

The type of head is not unlike those of the great dogs which have pricked ears, and collars, that are carved on the ivory handle of the predynastic stone knife found in Egypt, now in the Louvre.

Plate 14 shows how skilfully the Rhynes have been arranged to draw the construction of the Hound's head but does not show the eye below the well-marked brow (its place is indicated on the accompanying illustration); the air view supplies this deficiency, for two large circles appear on the photo either side of the Rhyne that divides the second from the third field south west from the brow; they are not visible on the ground.

On a hot 1st of May, golden glossy King Cups (marsh marigolds) bloom on this sleeping eye, which looked West, that is, straight down the nave of St. Michael's Chapel, with its foundations in the form of a cross on the top of the prehistoric Mount; the **High History** says "she goeth to the cross" when speaking of the questing hound.

Collinson's **History of Somerset** remarks concerning this St. Michael's Mount: "It had its name from a large borough or mount, very high and steep, which, though generally reckoned natural, seems to have been thrown up by hands for the purpose of a sepulchral tumulus. This opinion is corroborated by the many battles which are known to have been fought in these parts in very early times, the tradition of the inhabitants, and the instruments of war which have been found in its vicinity unsimilar to those of modern ages. Add to this, the materials of which this borough is composed are such as are not to be found within less than three miles of the place, viz.: at Red Hill, within the parish of Currey Rivel, being a stiff, very deep red clay. This mound stands on the East side of the river Parrett . . . At high water, when the tide is in, the river is sixty feet wide and eighteen deep, and coal barges of forty or fifty tons easily come up it." That was written in 1791.

The river Tone flows past the Isle of Athelney into the Parrett, under the Hound's watering mouth; cakes used to be fed to The famous dog, hence possibly the story that 'King Alfred burnt the cakes at Athelney,' a persistent legend believed in here, that seems to have no point otherwise.

As in **The High History of the Holy Graal** "the lord of the hold" is called "of Little Gomeret," it may be of interest to quote Godfrey Higgins; he says that it was the Gomerions "who brought the Tauric festival to Britain," and that "Gomer was the son of one of the first men who escaped the flood;" also that "According to all ancient histories the Cimbri and Picti were Gomerions."

Bearing on the same subject Colonel Waddell remarks in **Phœnician Origin of Britons,** page 195:

"On the south is Somerset or 'Seat of the Somers, Sumers or Cymyrs;' and the western promontory at the Severn mouth is 'Hercules Point,' the 'Herakles Akron' of Ptolemy (or modern 'Hart-land Point'), indicating the former presence of the Hercules-worshipping Phœnician navigating colonists there. The Upper Severn rises in Mount-Gomery, which name is now seen to mean 'The Mount of the Cymry, Somers, or 'Gomers'—the latter being also the Hebrew form of the ethnic name 'Sumer.'

This information should give some idea of the age of the effigy Hound, who we have seen was the wife of Marin the Jealous of Little Gomeret.

It is so far outside the ring of Zodiacal effigies that no stars correspond with it.

"The Questing Beast"

In Branch 17 of the **High History** we read, that "the questing beast" gives birth to twelve hounds that tear her with their teeth "but no power had they to devour her flesh," which suggests that she was made before the twelve zodiacal effigies, if they were her pups.

Also Malory in **Le Morte D'Arthur** says that after King Arthur's dream when "Him thought there was come into this land griffins and serpents" . . . "the king saw coming towards him the strangest beast that ever he saw or heard of; so the beast went to the well and drank, and the noise was in the beast's belly like unto the questing of thirty couple hounds; and all the while the beast drank there was no noise in the beast's belly."

It will be seen on the map that the Hound's mouth is called Moon's Drove; the tides being governed by the moon, whilst she drank of them "there was no noise;" but at spring tide the difference between low and high water in the Parrett estuary is occasionally 'fifty feet,' then the roar of the tidal bore is loudest when it reaches her "belly," and the noise of it is "like unto the questing of thirty couple hounds."

The thirty couple mentioned twice, perhaps refer this time to the thirty days and nights of the month, for all these beasts have some connection with the calendar.

THE EFFIGY HEAD OF CANIS MINOR

The High History of the Holy Graal. Branch 12. Title 4.

When Perceval "came to seek the shield, the brachet, that had remained in the hall, played gladly with him and went away with him."

In representations relating to the worship of Mithra, besides the Signs of the Zodiac, a little dog is shown leaping up to lick the Bull's wound; it figures largely in this "Romance" as Meliot of Logres, for we know now that all King Arthur's knights have their stellar counterpart.

The well-known star Procyon in Canis Minor, when pricked through from the Planisphere on the circular map of the Temple of the Stars, falls by this Little Dog's collar at Littleton, near the Lion's paw, hence the association in the **History** of the child Meliot with the Lion. The other star Gomeisa falls on its collar.

Around the place where these stars fall extensive Roman remains were excavated about a hundred years ago by Samuel Hasell who lived there; possibly it was a Mithraic settlement.

West Hill, close to the river Cary, forms the head of this little effigy. Canis Minor amongst the Euphrates constellations was a water dog, but the Arabs included it in their huge Lion sign.

Branch 24. Titles 6 and 7, speak of its relation to the Griffon which is on the other side of the river thus :

"the griffins love her as much as one beast may love another, and have such joy and such desire to play with the brachet that they will leave you alone."

Probably the legend was known at Wells in 1174 A.D., for on the North Porch of the Cathedral, the Griffon, half bird, half lion, is carved in stone, opposite to a child leading a Lion.

On the east side of West Hill, by the Little Dog's eye, stood the fine Romano-British Villa of which a plan is given in the **Victoria County History**, showing three hypocausts, baths, and a Bacchus pavement among other mosaics; it seems to have been nearly 250 feet long from east to west.

The baths were supplied by Bradley spring that never varies in the longest drought and still waters hundreds of acres beyond the villa by means of the ancient water ways. Perhaps it is to this spring the Giant Orion points with the finger that is now Redland Cottage garden.

There is so much about Meliot of Logres, his Hall and his Lion, in the **High History,** that we can only quote the following, which is important as giving the clue to his canine parentage, i.e. the great Hound of the Parrett river just described:

Branch 5. Title 1.

"And Messire Gawain looketh at the child that rode upon the lion right fainly. 'Sir,' saith the hermit, 'None durst guard him or be master over him save this child only, and yet the lad is not more than six years of age.

Sir, he is of right noble lineage, albeit he is the son of the most cruel man and most felon that is. Marin the Jealous is his father, that slew his wife on account of Messire Gawain."

The **History** tells us that both Meliot and his mother were of Logres.

West Hill is perhaps the most comprehensive and accessible viewpoint here, for Bradley Hill to the south forms the Griffon Bird's wing; to the west the singular outline of Lollover Hill silhouettes the hip and stomach of the Giant Orion, Dundon Hill close by showing the top of his great head. Further north Collard Hill forms the Bull's neck, with the clear cut outline of its ear and horns pointing to the south east. Just across the Compton to Littleton road due east, lies the Lion's tongue, "red beard" and flat jaw-bone above, whilst his paw—Castley Hill—dominates Littleton.

We now see why Meliot was of such importance that he was called "of Logres;" in the midst of these hills and red cliffs he lies in the so-called "cave" of this Giant Fairyland, which is perhaps more beautiful wrapped in profound sleep, than when "The bull bellowed so passing loud that right unearth was it to hear ought else within the castle besides" and, "The Lion gave out a roar so loud that all the forest resounded thereof."

117

CHAPTER XI

ARGO NAVIS

THE SHIP OF THE SUN THAT SAILS INTO THE WEST

The High History of the Holy Graal. Branch 35. Title 2.
"So soon as the ship had taken haven under the castle,
the sea withdraweth itself back, so that the ship is left on
dry land."

Branch 12. Title 3.
"The ship was arrived under the palace and was quite
still. When the ship had taken ground, the King looketh
thereat with much marvelling."

The Ship that had "taken haven" is three miles long; its main mast is
over one mile, but the after mast, called **Sale Piece,** is less than a mile in
length being raised on the poop, which resembles that of a fourth dynasty
Egyptian boat (see page 393, Maspero's **Dawn of Civilization**).

On Street Moor lies the main sail "with the Red Cross thereon," for
Aldebaran of the Royal Star Cross falls just above in the Bull's bell.

Branch 35. Title 27.
"Perceval heard one day a bell sound loud and high
without the manor toward the sea. He came to the windows
of the hall and saw the ship come with the white sail and
the Red Cross thereon, and within were the fairest folk that
ever he might behold, and they were all robed in such
manner as though they should sing mass. When the ship
was anchored under the hall they went to pray in the most
holy chapel."

The strange thing about the whole craft is that whereas all the
giant creatures described in these notes are drawn with living curves,
this inanimate object is depicted by perfectly straight lines suggestive
of planks of wood in its construction; it lies on its side, whilst the hills
forming Orion the Giant rise out of it, rather in the shape of an acorn
from its cup.

The bottom of the boat is outlined by Walton Drove (the keel by
Pitney Stert Drove), the whole framework being delineated by water
dykes called 'rhynes.'

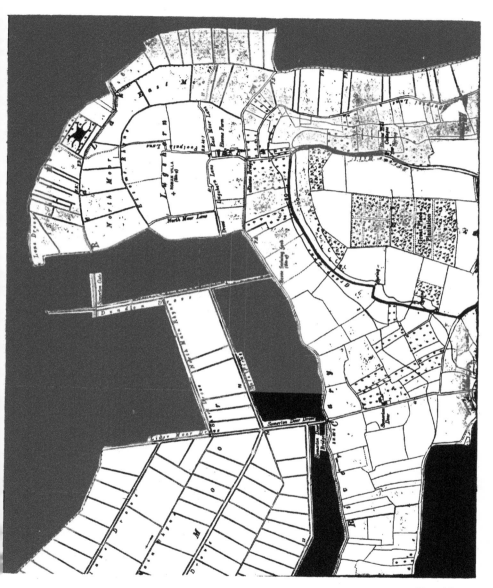

"GRIFFON" BIRD and POOP of SHIP

119

Plate 15

'The Phantom Ship'

For King Solomon's Ship see Malory's "Morte D'Arthur." Book 17. Chap. 5, 6, & 7.

The custom of parading the Sailor's horse at Minehead—which place can be seen from the top of Dundon Beacon—lends colour to the legend of King Solomon's Ship.

Every year from the first to the third day of May, an imitation inverted **boat** is dressed up as a hobby horse whose stable is down in the old Quay: its houseling is painted with circular spots.

It is said locally that the custom commemorates the advent of "a sort of Phantom Ship which entered the Harbour without captain or crew in remote times."

Most enlightening is the fact that it always used to have a real cow's tail; (in remembrance of Taurus).

The head is a mask of a horse wearing a conical hat, surmounted by a peacock feather; (the builder of the heavenly Argo Navis was represpented by a peacock).

Other Hobby horses had "snappers" covered with hare's skin and hare's ears attached; (in the effigy ship the constellation Lepus is the Giant's seat).

One of the verses that is sung during the prancing of the horse is:

"Awake. St. George, our English knight Oh!
For summer is acome and winter is ago,
And every day God gives us His grace,
By day and night Oh!"

The horse crouches down during the verse, and at the end springs up leaping into the air, like the sun at sunrise.

In Salisbury Museum can be seen a Giant with his Hobby Horse; they used to be taken out every St. John's day, the 24th June, which is the Giant Orion's month. John the Baptist is especially connected with the Grail legends, and the **High History** says that it being St. John's day "the son of King Urien served that day at the Table before the King. Orion was first spelt Urion according to the **Classical Dictionary.**

Branch 12. Title 3.

"He looked at it until he espied what seemed him to be a ship wherein was the light, and he was minded not to move until such time as he should know whether a ship it were or something other. The longer he looketh at it, the better perceiveth he that it is a ship, and that it was coming with great rushing toward the castle as fast as it might. The King espieth it nigh at hand, but none seeth he within nor without save one old man, ancient and bald, of right passing seemliness that held the rudder of the ship.

The mast of Orion's ship (this ship of the sun that sails into the West), is worthy of attention as it may have suggested the May Pole or Sun Pole, from which streamed down the rays that are represented by ribbons in the country dance; for it marked the May Equinox 2700 B.C., and in that case took the place of the pole star Tree of Life, which Pole was not decked with streamers, but had a circular Garland round the top, and others hung on pegs lower down.

The stars of the sky river Eridanus fall on the vessel, and stars from Columba fall on the rudder by the Griffon bird's claws.

At the present day, the effigy Ship carries corn amongst other produce, but during the drought of 1934 the ship was on fire for more than a month, the soil being peat.

T. W. Rolleston's **Myths and Legends of the Celtic Race** gives some interesting illustrations of solar ship-carvings of the Megalithic People, notably one at New Grange, Ireland; and H. J. Massingham in his **Downland Man,** page 76, reproduces drawings of three boats, one from Lake Victoria, one from Egypt, and one from rock carvings in Sweden, all terminating in a ram's head. The bow of the effigy boat here touches the effigy Aries, just below the Corn Mill.

From time to time great balks of wood are brought to the surface on this effigy boat. Taunton Castle Museum has some preserved.

THE HAWK or "GRIFFON"
THAT STANDS ON THE RUDDER OF ORION'S SHIP

"Thou dost sink down and make an end of the hours."

Gemini is an air sign, and as Orion is here one of the Twins, the bird that faces him should be the other twin; Canis Major on the Egyptian Zodiac of the 'Grand Portico' in the Temple at Dendera is represented by a similar bird standing next to Orion's boat, and as all the stars of Canis Major correspond with this effigy when pricked through from the planisphere, some kind of Egyptian influence is certainly indicated. But I do not think this effigy is contemporary with the others.

The Egyptian 'Bronze Falcon's Head' reproduced in colour on post cards at the British Museum, strangely resembles this one in outline.

The Dendera bird is crowned; it will be remembered that the crown of the **High History** was given by King Arthur to Sir Perceval, and also promised to him by the Master, and this hawk-headed creature may have been one of Perceval's effigies.

The tail of the bird lies between the paws of the Lion, as if he were springing on to its back; it thus suggests the composite Griffon, half lion, half bird; it was in this effigy that the Castle of the Griffons lay that Sir Lancelot visited more than once in peril of his life. See Branch 24. Titles 6 and 7.

Branch 30. Title 7.
> "But, had he known where it was he had come, little sleep would he have had, for he was close to the cavern where he slew the lion and where the griffons were, that had come in from the forest all gorged of victual, and were fallen on sleep, and it was for them that the postern-gate had been left unbolted. A damsel went down from a chamber by a trap-door with a brachet on her arm for fear of the griffons, and as she went toward the postern-gate to lock it she espied Lancelot, that lay asleep in the midst of the orchard."

The brachet on her arm was Canis Minor close by, and the postern-gate Somerton Gate.

On the poop of the Ship lies Liver Moor Drove, which explains why the Griffons were "gorged of victual:" perhaps one of them was the bird that Hercules shot for eating the liver of Prometheus, brother of Atlas. In any case it might be said with Homer—"The immortal liver grows and gives the immortal feast."

The important star Sirius, when transferred from the planisphere to the map, corresponds with two springs below Bradley Hill, lying on the edge of the Griffon bird's left wing.

The Cary river, after delineating the effigies of Virgo and Leo, outlines the back and front of this bird creature of the ship, supplying the water to that vessel also: the under part of the body and the back of the leg is drawn by Bancombe Road and Park Lane as far as the footpath from Park Farm to Stepping Stones. The footpath and the river then outline the bird's claws.

Somerton Door Bridge leads by Somerton Door Drove along the poop of the ship, to the knees of the Giant Orion.

A Roman villa is marked on the six-inch O.S. sheet 63 S.W. at Lugshorn (Lug meaning God of Light), it stood in the head of the effigy, which is outlined by two artificial loops of the Cary river; this is interesting, as it was the Griffon Head that is so specially mentioned in the **History.** "The head of one of them shall he take and bring to me at Castle Perilous." The beak, formed by South Moor, has an enclosure of banks on its tip by Hayes Lane Drove, at which the Giant Orion seems to gaze with his now sightless eye, or at his own solar plexus.

Dundon Drove leads from this small enclosure to Grove Steining Ford, which is another ancient name meaning the stone ford of the Druid's sacred Grove, for the star Sirius falls on Grove Lane.

Somerton Gate is the name of the breach in the great artificial embankment partly outlining Red Lake. The two place-names Door and Gate imply an important approach to Lollover and Dundon Hills.

The glassy eye of the Griffon, which is formed by a decoy pond, is worth noting: it can be seen in the orchard by Decoy Farm, enclosed by four dykes; perhaps it is meant for a double eye.

So much labour has been expended in making it, and in digging all the other ancient waterways of the Sacred Area, that on the principle that one can only take out of a thing what has been put in to it, it is no

123

wonder "they had such great abundance there within of everything they could desire, that nought in the world was there whereof they lacked." For this they gave the credit to the Bull close by.

The rudder of the ship, on which the great bird stands, is connected to the keel by Pitney Stert Bridge leading from Straight Drove to the well-known Pitney Roman Villa.

This Villa, which was built round a court and measured 325 ft. from east to west, and 210 ft. from north to south, was excavated by Mr. Hasell in 1828, and is described with other Roman remains by Sir R. C. Hoare in his privately printed **Pitney Pavement**; the book is in the Taunton Museum Library. **The Somerset Victoria County History** gives a plan of the Villa, and illustration of its mosaic floor; but all is now buried under the green sod.

The symbols held by the numerous figures in these elaborate pavements are unusual, and also the subjects. A single nude figure in the centre of one design, represents a youth about to kill a snake with a weapon he is holding over his head: perhaps he is meant for Orion who, according to Ovid, "died of the bite of a scorpion which the earth produced, to punish his vanity in boasting that there was not on earth any animal which he could not conquer." Out of the tub that the youth holds, articles like coins are falling. Another figure in a pointed cap is said to be Mithra.

There is a second Roman Villa marked on the map close to this one, and there are sites of two more on Starwell Tree Hill, besides the one near Sam's Cross above Low Ham. In fact a dozen or more partly excavated Romanized dwellings, and "30 acres" of Roman remains are known to lie around this effigy.

The Pitney Villa and one at Littleton were found to have been centrally heated; a mass of lead pipes from them and other remains, including 'a basin of Parian marble,' were for long preserved in Mr. Straddling's Museum at Chilton Polden with an inscribed Roman stone from the Pitney Villa, described in the **County History,** now in Bridgwater Museum; some of the other relics were sent to Taunton Museum, whilst gipsies destroyed what remained.

Lug God of Light

But why did a highly civilized people settle on this stretch of the

Cary river two thousand years ago, and a Bronze Age race leave their flint implements on the sea sand bank near Grey Lake Fosse close by? (These worked flints are well illustrated in the April 1933 number of Man). It may be that they worshipped the god of Dundon, Lug god of Light, judging from the place-name Lugs-horn.

Those interested in sun worship would do well to turn up Mithras in the **Encyclopædia Britannica,** for though in the time of the Roman Conquest of Britain that Persian religion of vast antiquity had been debased, it probably lingered here.

Roman soldiers stationed at Caerleon were Mithra worshippers for a Mithra temple was found at Caerleon, just across the Severn Sea.

One degree in the System of Mithra was the Gryphon, others were the Lion, the Ox, the Eagle, the Sun, etc.: and as this creature compounded of lion and bird was consecrated to the sun, and watched over mines of gold and hidden treasure (according to the **Imperial Dictionary)** it is worth rescuing from oblivion.

Branch 33. Title 6.

" 'Meliot,' saith Messire Gawain, 'See you, there is Perceval the Good Knight, and now may we say of a truth that he is in sore peril of death; for that ship, save God bethink Him thereof, shall arrive in such manner and in such a place as that never more shall we have no witting of him.' "

Branch 35. Title 2.

"None were therein save Perceval, his horse, and the pilot. They issued forth of the ship and went by the side of the sea toward the castle, and therein were the fairest halls and the fairest mansions that any might see ever."

By killing Chaos the Red and the Red Knight of the red shield, when still a lad, Perceval won back this "castle" which had belonged to the Widow Lady his mother (the moon), it thus appears to have been Sir Perceval's effigy before he took possession of the Phœnix of the Isle of Avalon. (Wolfram von Echenbach confirms the conjecture.)

La Queste del Saint Graal graphically describes his experience on the "Island" rock in chapter 6, page 76 of W. W. Comfort's translation,

125

but says later "then Perceval leaned on the rail of the boat with the good man," and, "the lion kept close beside him wagging his tail," which would apply to this Griffon effigy next to the Lion.

As the Dove near the Serpent is also associated with Perceval, we suppose that he stood for the element Air, and the Spirit of the Sun, and was thus the 'Twin' to Orion.

> "Sometimes on lonely mountain-meres
>   I find a magic bark;
> I leap on board: no helmsman steers;
>   I float till all is dark.
>
> Oh, blessed vision! blood of God!
>   My spirit beats her mortal bars,
> As down dark tides the glory slides,
>   And star-like mingles with the stars."
>
> Tennyson's **Sir Galahad.**

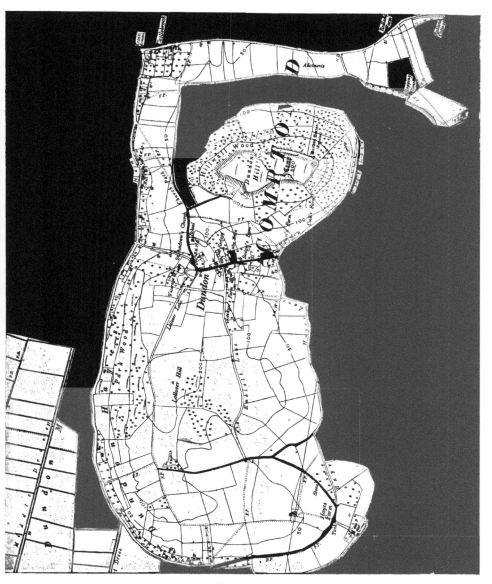

ORION

Plate 16

THE GIANT LOGRIN, here one of the "Twins."

127

CHAPTER XII

ORION THE GIANT

"Uru-Anna, Light of Heaven;" and Sun God of the Phœnicians.

JUNE

The High History of the Holy Graal. Branch 6. Title 4.

" 'Sir,' saith Messire Gawain, 'Wherefore make the folk of this castle such dole, and they of all this land and all this country? For I hear them weep and beat their palms together on every side.' 'Sir,' saith he, 'I will tell you. King Gurgalain had one only son of whom he hath been bereft by a Giant that hath done him many mischiefs and wasted much of his land.' "

Orion was once the most celebrated of all the Giants, and the stars of his constellation correspond with the body of his effigy, when transferred from the planisphere to the map of Dundon and Lollover Hills: he was probably the oldest and most important of all the Nature gods in this Temple of the Stars.

The Stars of Orion

Rigel on his right leg,

Betelgeuze on left shoulder,

Bellatrix on chest,

His belt on stomach,

Sword below belt,

Saiph on left knee.

The Stars of Orion

Orion takes the place of one of the Twins in Somerset; two of the stars of that constellation fall on his right hand, and he is the house of the Sun which was Twin to the Moon. In Egypt he figured both as Osiris and Horus, whilst in Persian representations of Gemini, Orion himself or his giant head is shown between the Twins.

The effigy Orion looks as if he were supporting the Round Table of the Somerset Zodiac on his right arm like Atlas, who, Homer says, "keeps the tall pillars which hold heaven and earth asunder;" these pillars were thought to rest in the western sea. Atlas was said to own the Garden of the Hesperides, and was turned into a rocky mountain.

The Giant's uplifted arm, which is bent in the form of a Mason's square, is superbly outlined by the road from Compton to Redlands Farm, beneath which the hand lies, with the tip of the thumb touching Stepping Stones, and two fingers almost meeting it as if holding something.

The bend at the elbow is marked by the remains of an ancient cross at Castlebrook Hamlet, so called in reference to the pre-historic camp or castle on Dundon Hill, supplied by a spring, that has now been diverted.

Branch 16. Title 2.

" 'From what land hath come such manner of man?'
'Sir,' say the knights, 'He is come from the Giant's castle, and he warreth upon you for the love of Logrin the Giant.' "

Looking up from the Cross, the camp, seen against the sky, draws the outline of the back of the Giant's ear, for his head lies half buried in the ground, whilst this right ear listens to the music of the spheres.

Considering that his face—which looks down west—is three-quarters of a mile long from the point of the chin to the top of the head, it is a marvellous work of art: the jaw is finely drawn by the flagstones called Church Path; and though the lips and tip of the nose have been obliterated by the houses of Dundon village, the Tithe Barn is still in his mouth.

Branch 6. Title 5.

"the enclosure of the mountain went round about for a good three leagues Welsh, and therewithin was the Giant, so great and cruel and horrible that he feared no man in the world, and for a long time had he not been sought out by any knight, for none durst won in that quarter."

Lempriere's Classical Dictionary says that Orion laid himself down to sleep on the seashore; when he awoke he found his eye had been put out, but when he turned his face towards the rising sun he immediately recovered his eyesight. Other giants, including the first Horus, seem to have been afflicted in the same way. Nevertheless, though almost obscured, the eyeball can just be made out not far from Dundon Smithy, by the entrance to the newly planted orchard, whence the modelling of the brow is apparent, with the magnificent forehead beyond.

As for the ear—formed by the camp—its enormous size is reminiscent of the ears of Eastern gods; a prehistoric stone embankment outlines its edge, whilst a tumulus on the tip is called Dundon Beacon. This tumulus was opened about a hundred years ago, but unfortunately no record kept, other than that it contained humain remains; until recently the Beacon fire was regularly lighted there on great occasions.

The entrance to this ancient Sanctuary of the ear is opposite St. Andrew's Church, whence the path, having outlined the under part of the jaw, leads up a steep incline to the defaced ear-hole. Many worked flints and bronze rings used to be picked up close by, but nothing has been found recently.

From this isolated hill, which is 300 ft. above King's Sedge Moor, there is a fine view on clear days, and sometimes incredibly beautiful sunsets: it is a superb situation for an altar to the setting sun.

Vedic Hymn
"Sacred fire! Purifying fire! Thou who sleepest in wood and mountest in shining flames on the altar, thou art the heart of sacrifice, the fearless aspiration of prayer, the Divine spark concealed in all things, and the glorious Soul of the Sun."

Branch 6. Title 5.

"He is come to level ground and looketh before him and seeth a hold that the Giant had on the top of a rock, and espieth the Giant and the lad where they were sitting on the level ground under a tree."

The Giant "thinketh to carry him to his hold that was within the rock. And as he goeth thither he falleth, Missire Gawain and all, and he lieth undermost. Howbeit he thinketh to rise, but cannot, for Messire Gawain sendeth him his sword right through his heart and beyond."

Lollover Hill forms the Giant's body, small in comparison with the head and consequently suggestive of a child or dwarf. He is seated in profile on what the Arabs called 'the chair of the Giant'—i.e., the constellation Lepus—in the pose of a cross-legged Buddha.

On the Giant's ribs is an interesting specimen of 'cultivation lynch'
130

modelling, indicating the costal cartilages of the lower ribs of the right side, they are visible in the air photograph. The nasty wound on the groin is as red and lacerated as ever!—it is shown in the illustration, which is inserted due east and west.

The rest of the anatomy is admirably delineated by Ham Lane, running west all round his back, and by Emblett Lane and Hayes Lane in front, whilst Hayes Farm stands on his right knee; it is astonishing that such fine drawing could have lasted so long.

The highest part of the hill, between the aforesaid wound and the ribs, is 295 ft. above Orion's Ship, already described.

At a remote date Lollover Hill was washed by sea waves that are now kept out of the Moors by walls and locks.

It is lamentable that the three Stones marked on the former O.S. Sheets 63 N.W. were removed and broken up by a stranger; the fragments are still in the barn close by the field, called Above Groats, in which they lay. The Stones apparently had no signs upon them, but the field, which is never ploughed, has shallow trenches that cross each other and are not necessary for drainage. The pond in the lower corner is full of water in the longest drought; a little flag-stoned bridge passed beside it, whence water could be drawn.

The star Bellatrix, when pricked through from the planisphere on to the map, falls where the three Stones lay on the Giant's chest or heart, by Lockyer's Farm.

It has been said that the Iberian type lingered at Dundon longer than anywhere else in the neighbourhood, and until these historic hills changed hands, the ancient landmarks and traditions were sacred; a quotation from Jacob Bryant may be in place here, he says: "The Iberians of Baetica seem to have delighted in a kind of dirge, and funeral music. Hence they are said by Philostratus to have been the only people in the world, who celebrated the triumphs of death."

The stars of "the scabbard" of Orion's famous sword, when transferred from the planisphere to the map, lie below his stomach on Hayes Lane; but Red Lake earthwork is perhaps meant by "the sword came forth thereof all bloody" for it extends from his thumb downwards; it is over a mile long and more like a snake than the sword, which is described in the following:

Branch 6. Title 4.

"Then the King draweth it forth of the scabbard, and the sword came forth thereof all bloody, for it was the hour of noon. And he made hold it before Messire Gawain until the hour was past, and thereafter the sword becometh as clear as an emerald and as green."

The Giant's Head

Now let us consider the name of the Giant's head—for heads play such an important part in the **High History**—it is called Dun Don or Fort of Don. Geoffrey Higgins says in **The Anacalypsis**, "We have before seen that when we pursued the word Don to the utmost point to which we could carry our researches, we found it to end in Wisdom."

Don, Euron, and Euronwy—Edward Davies tells us in **Mythology and Rites of the British Druids**—was a mystical personage; he says: "Amongst the ancient poems relating to this mystical personage I must distinguish one which is entitled Cadair Ceridwen:" "When the merit of the presidencies shall be adjudged mine will be found the superior amongst them—my chair, my cauldron, and my laws, and my pervading eloquence, meet for the presidency. I am accounted skilful in the Court of Don."

Not only is the Giant's head a fort of wisdom, but presumably a symbol of the setting sun towards which twelve of the effigies are represented as looking.

Branch 19. Titles 1 and 2.

"The messenger cometh back again and saith thereof that two suns appear to be shining, the one in the East and the other in the West. He marvelleth much thereat, and prayeth Our Lord that he may be permitted to know wherefore two suns should appear in such wise."

"Straightway behold you, a damsel that cometh" bearing Lohot's head.

Branch 19. Title 6.

" 'These letters say that the knight whose head lieth in this vessel was named Lohot, and he was son of King Arthur and Queen Guenievre. He had slain on a day that is past, Logrin the Giant, by his hardiment. Messire Kay the

Seneschal was passing by there, and so found Lohot sleeping upon Logrin, . . . The King himself maketh dole thereof so sore that none may comfort him, for before these tidings he had thought that his son was still on live and that he was the Best Knight in the world, . . never did no man see greater dole made in the King's court than they of the Table Round made for the youth.' "

Branch 15. Title 7, says, previous to the above :

" 'Meseemed that the corpse lay therewithin for whom the service was ordained.' 'You say truth,' saith the hermit. 'I have done it for Lohot, King Arthur's son, that lieth buried under this pall.' "

Undoubtedly the secret of the original Grail lies in that statement "for whom the service was ordained," hence the wailing of the women that haunts the **High History,** by which sign Perceval "bethought him what folk they might be." (Branch 9. Title 11.)

We have shown that King Arthur's effigy was the giant Hercules representing the sun in the east; the effigy of his son Lohot was the giant Orion representing the sun in the west, for Lohot's head enters Arthur's hall just as the "two suns" are seen shining, "the one in the East," "the other in the West." In the corners of the "Glaston clock" in Wells Cathedral, four giant heads represent the sun in the four Quarters.

Speaking of Lohot, the **High History** tells us that he was the giant :

" 'I marvel much,' saith the King, 'what hath become of him, for no tidings have I heard of him beyond these, that Kay the Seneschal slew Logrin the giant.' " (Branch 12. Title 1.)

Giants, "Born of Heaven and Earth"

As for the origin of the giant effigies, **The History of the Kings of Britain,** by Geoffrey of Monmouth, on page 14 of the Everyman's edition, says :

"Brute, past the realms of Gaul, beneath the sunset
Lieth an Island, girt about by ocean,
Guarded by ocean, **erst the haunt of giants,**
Desert of late, and meet for this thy people,
Seek it! for there is thine abode for ever."

133

And again on page 20:

"At that time the name of the island was Albion, and of none was it inhabited save only of a few giants."

From the above statements it is clear that the Giants—i.e. Nature gods "born of Heaven and Earth" (for no giant skeletons have been found)—did exist in Albion long before Brutus the Trojan came to Britain about B.C. 1103, to the land that had been 'erst the haunt of giants.'

So the "question" is now, not, "unto whom one serveth of the Grail?" —for it was served originally to the supreme God of the Starry Universe, the Bardic sign for whom was OIV—but, who were those who served it first? Who made the Giants? Whose was the consummate genius that could see in these rivers and hills a complex circular design, and having envisaged it as a Zodiac, command such skilled labour to carry it out that the stars of the Ecliptic Circle, as well as those of Orion and Hercules fit the composition to a nicety? and if regularly interlaced equilateral triangles—representing earth, fire, water and air—are laid on the centre of the circle of Giants, their twelve apexes point to their respective effigies.

The drawing of the effigies is free, powerful, realistic, not in any way conventionalized; the effigies definitely indicate a Sanctuary made by star-gazers, who were practical enough to apply their scientific religion to fructifying Mother Earth by natural methods of irrigation; when the knights were unable to ask that vital question, the temple waterways became neglected and drought ensued, as the History states.

Such a Caer Sidi of living science and art could only have emanated from a highly imaginative people of profound experience and vitality; whose God was 'immanent' not only in their daily Mass of food and drink, and in the very ground upon which they trod, but permanently pervading the Universe around them.

Rhys Brydydd sang:

"The smallest of the small is Hu the Mighty, in the world's judgment; yet he is the greatest, and Lord over us, we sincerely believe, and our God of mystery. Light is his course, and swift, a particle of lucid sunshine is his car. He is great on land and seas—the greatest whom I shall behold—greater than the worlds! Let us beware of offering mean indignity to HIM, the Great and the Bountiful!"

Mythology and Rites of the British Druids, page 110.

That is the Bardic conception of their god Hu, the worship of whom was carried from the "Summer Country" to the "Isle of Britain" in "the age of ages," according to the Sixth Triad.

"Let the rock beyond the billow be set in order at the dawn, displaying the countenance of him who receives the exile into his sanctuary — the rock of the supreme proprietor, the chief place of tranquility." In the name of this rock the mystic priest proclaims: *"I am the cell, I am the opening chasm, I am the place of re-animation!"*

Mythology and Rites of the British Druids, page 163.

*   *   *   *   *   *

As we close, a gigantic double rainbow spans the entrance to the Temple of the Stars, forming a gateway of glowing colours reflected from the Setting Sun.

BIBLIOGRAPHY

B

Balch, H. E.	The Caves of Mendip	Folk Press Ltd.
Bothwell-Gosse, A.	The Knights Templars	J. M. Watkins
Brown, Robert. Jun.	Primitive Constellations	Williams and Norgate
Bryant, Jacob	A new System or an Analysis of Ancient Mythology. 1774-6	
Budge, E. A. Wallis	The Nile. 1912	Thos. Ccok and Sons
Bulleid, Arthur	The Lake Villages of Somerset	Folk Press Ltd.
Burrow, Edward J.	Ancient Earthworks and Camps of Somerset	Ed. J. Burrow and Co.

C

Collinson, John	The History and Antiquities of the County of Somerset. 1791	
Comfort, W. Wister	The Quest of the Holy Grail, translated from the Old French	J. M. Dent and Sons

D

Davis, Edward	The Mythology and Rites of the British Druids. 1809	J. Booth
Dobson, D. P.	The Archaeology of Somerset. 1931	Methuen and Co.

E

	Encyclopaedia Britannica. 11th Edition	Cambridge University Press
Evans, Sebastian	The High History of the Holy Graal, translated from the Old French	J. M. Dent and Sons

G

Geden, A. S.	Mithraism	Society for Promoting Christian Knowledge
Geoffrey of Monmouth	Histories of the Kings of Britain. Everyman's Library.	J. M. Dent and Sons

H

Higgins, Godfrey	Anacalypsis	
Higgins, Godfrey	The Celtic Druids. 1827	R. Hunter
Hill, S. E.	Astrology: The Link between Two Worlds	John M. Watkins
Hoare, R. C.	Pitney Pavement. 1832	
Hutton, Edward	Highways and Byways in Somerset	Macmillan

I

Ithel, J. Williams AB	Barddas. The Bardo-Druidic System of the Isle of Britain. Translations and Notes. 1862.	Longman and Co.

L

Lempriere, John	A Classical Dictionary	George Routledge and Sons
Lewis, Rev. Lionel	St. Joseph of Arimathea at Glastonbury	The Avalon Press
Lomax, Frank	The Antiquities of Glastonbury by William of Malmesbury	Talbot: 13, Paternoster Row, London

M

Mackenzie, Donald — Indian Myth and Legend — The Gresham Publishing Co.

Malory, Thomas — Le Morte d'Arthur. 1903 — Macmillan and Co.

Maspero, G. — Dawn of Civilisation — Society for Promoting Christian Knowledge

Massingham, H. J. — How Ball Games Began. 1832 — The Listener

Merejkowski, Dmitri — The Forerunner — Constable

O

Olcott, William Tyler — Star Lore of All Ages — G. P. Putnam's Sons

Olcott, William Tyler — Sun Lore of All Ages — G. P. Putnam's Sons

Oxford Dictionary

P

Perry, W. J. — The Children of the Sun. 1923 — Methuen

Plunket, Emmeline M. — Ancient Calendars and Constellations. 1903 — John Murray

Pope, Alexander — The Iliad and Odyssey of Homer — Frederick Warne and Co.

R

Rawlinson, George — History of Phoenicia. 1889 — Longmans, Green and Co.

Rhys, John — The Hibbert Lectures. 1886 — Williams and Norgate

Rhys, John — Celtic Folklore — The Clarendon Press, Oxford

Robertson, J. Armitage (Late Dean of Wells) — Two Glastonbury Legends — Cambridge University Press

Rolleston, T. W. — Myths and Legends of the Celtic Race. 1911 — George G. Harrap and Co.

S

Schliemann, Henry — Ilios. The City and Country of The Trojans. 1880 — John Murray

Skeat, W. W. — Malay Magic. 1900 — Macmillan and Co.

Spence, Lewis — An Encyclopaedia of Occultism. 1920 — George Routledge and Sons

T

Taylor, C. — The Shepherd of Hermas — Society for Promoting Christian Knowledge

Tennyson, Alfred, Lord — The Works of Alfred Tennyson. 1896 — Macmillan

Tiddy, R. J. E. — Mummers' Plays

V

Victoria County History: Somerset. 2 vol. 1906, 1911. — Constable

W

Wace and Layamon — Arthurian Chronicles — J. M. Dent and Sons

Waddell, L. A. — Phoenician Origin of Britons, Scots and Anglo-Saxons — Williams and Norgate

Waddell, L. A. — The British Edda — Chapman and Hall

Ward, J. S. M. — An Outline History of Freemasonry — The Baskerville Press

Wolfram von Eschenbach — Parzival. Translated by J. L. Weston. — David Nutt

Wright, Rev. G. N. — China. Engravings by T. Allom. 1843. 4 vol.

137

INDEX

of

SUBJECT HEADINGS

INTRODUCTION

Page

The chief characters of **The High History of the Holy Graal** and what they stand for   8

The Earth Chart of the Stars in Somerset. The list shows how the stars fall in
regard to their corresponding Nature Effigies..   9

"The Great Secrets"..   14

CHAPTER I. The Fire Sign, Leo....................   15

The Lion of the "forbidden land" of Logres..   15
"From the time of the coming of Brutus"...   15
The Arthurian Lion a Nature Effigy...   16
Other Constellation effigies outlined...   16
Somerton, the former Capital of Somerset...   17
From the left fore paw to the hind leg of the Lion...   19
An Alabaster Quarry on the Lion's Collar...   19
The Lion's Ears   20
The enchanted Springs of Logres...   20
Leo is personified by Lancelot...   21
A Mantle made of Beards..   21
The Grave-yard Perilous lies either side of the Lion's tail.................................   22
Somerton Lane is not a motor road..   23
The Lion's Head   23
Leo lies in Catsash Hundred...   24
"Miracles should not cease till the Great Lion had come".................................   24
The Sun Worshippers' Grave-Yard..   26
Leo's Solar Phases..   26

CHAPTER II. The Earth Sign, Virgo....................   29

She holds 'an ear of corn by a fall of water'...   29
Gates on the Sun's Path..   29
Her 'Kern-Baby'   30
The Cary River   31
"The paled bar"   31
"The Sepulchre"   32
Camelot..   34
Camelot's High-Altar   35
Three other Camels   36
The Ghostly Fire..   36

CHAPTER III. The Water Sign, Scorpio....................   39

"He was nigh his end being at the point of death"..   39
The river Brue flows through the Vale of Avalon...   40
The symbolic Human Head..   40
Lyd is said to mean Gate..   41

                                                                              Page
                        CHAPTER IV. The Fire Sign, Sagittarius..................... 43
Sagittarius is an ancient constellation figure.. 45
                        Hercules 'The King'.. 48
Ulysses sees Hercules in the Land of the Cimmerians......................... 48
King Arthur lies in the form of a St. George's Cross............................ 48
Glaston Twelve Hides 49
The Sun a Ball of Gold.. 50
The King's Hand 51
The glorious Hercules (King Arthur) of many lands........................... 53
Star Symbolism is traceable even to-day in many walks of life.......... 53

                        CHAPTER V. The Earth Sign, Capricornus................. 56
"The King of Castle Mortal".. 56
The Cave of the Rising?.. 57
Joseph the Tin Merchant.. 58

                        King Arthur's Queen.. 60

                        CHAPTER VI. The Air Sign, Aquarius...................... 63
The Water Bearer 63
The Universal Legend of the Cup of Immortality............................... 63
The Round Table of the Holy Grail is a Solar Wheel........................... 64
The Aquarius Moon Goblet described.. 64
The Five Cups that King Arthur beheld... 65
The Effigy Phoenix 65
The Tree of Life is the Pole Star "pillar;" the Royal Star Cross is the
    "cross of gold".. 66
The Crest of the Phoenix.. 67
The Effigies were purposely designed to be invisible, and now — the Key having
    been lost — can be traced only on the large scale Ordnance Survey Sheets, or
    from the air 68
The Castle that "never stinted of burning".. 68
The Effigy Creatures 69
The Archetypal Microcosm 71
Sir Perceval's Uncle called him "Par-lui-fet"...................................... 71
A land of Fire and Sun worship kindred to that of Egypt.................... 72
Did Actis of Heliopolis leave his name below the Tor? or is the land named after
    him? If so, why, and by whom?.. 72
Glastonbury Abbey's Pyramids, and her prehistoric Lake Villages.......... 73

                        CHAPTER VII. The Water Sign, Pisces and Cetus......... 76
The Sun beamed on all sides although the Night was dark.................... 78
The Line that ties the two Fishes on to the Whale............................... 79
The Castle of the Whale... 80

The Ancient Pole Star in Ursa Minor is Here Marked by a Serpent's Head on a "Crown,"
        Which was the Pole of this Temple of the Stars...................... 83
        The Great Finger of the Equinox Marks the Second Point of the
                        Suggested Triangle.. 87

Page

The Enclosure of the Sun the Apex of the Triangle............ 90

The Dove............ 94

CHAPTER VIII. The Fire Sign, Aries............ 97
Represented as a Lamb with head and fore foot reverted............ 97
Confirmation of the Effigy Constellations............ 99
The Tidal Port of the Kingdom of Logres............ 100
The Knights Templars the Guardians of the Grail............ 102

CHAPTER IX. The Earth Sign, Taurus............ 105
About 2700 B.C. the Vernal Equinox lay in the eye of the Bull............ 105
The Effigy............ 105
An Avenue of Cedars............ 106
The Bell............ 107
The Red Launde of Arthurian Romance............ 108
The Bull's Calf............ 109
The reason for not depicting more than the Bull's head and right foot............ 110

CHAPTER X. The Dogs............ 112
'The Dog of Gwyn ab Nudd, the British Pluto, is named Dor-Marth,' was it the great hound of the Parrett river?............ 112
"The Questing Beast"............ 115
Canis Minor............ 116

CHAPTER XI. Argo Navis............ 118
The Ship of the Sun that sails into the West............ 118
'The Phantom Ship'............ 120
Malory's Ship of King Solomon. (See Morte d'Arthur, Book 17, Chapters 5, 6 and 7)............ 120

The Hawk or "Griffon"............ 122
"The Griffon" that stands on the rudder of Orion's ship. The Hawk or Falcon was the Egyptian Canis Major............ 122
Lug god of Light............ 125

CHAPTER XII. The Giant Orion............ 128
"Uru-anna, Light of Heaven." The Sun god of the Phoenicians............ 128
The Giant's Head............ 132
Giants "born of Heaven and Earth"............ 133
Who made the Giants?............ 134